Family Managed, Multinationals and Public Sector Enterprises

The Strategic Choices for Global Competitiveness

Family Managed, Multinationals and Public Sector Enterprises

The Strategic Choices for Global Competitiveness

Ishwar Dayal
Mirza S. Saiyadain
Deepak Dogra
Kewal Sony
Poornima Gupta
Lubna Nafees

Ane Books Pvt. Ltd.
New Delhi ♦ Chennai

Family Managed, Multinationals and Public Sector Enterprises

Ishwar Dayal, Mirza S. Saiyadain, Deepak Dogra,
Kewal Sony, Poornima Gupta, Lubna Nafees

First Edition : 2007
Reprint : 2019, **2020**
Price: ₹ 295/-
Pages: viii + 156 =164 (Pb)
Size : Demy (5½" × 8½")

Published by

Ane Books Pvt. Ltd.

4821, Parwana Bhawan, 1st Floor, 24 Ansari Road, Darya Ganj,
New Delhi - 110 002, Tel.: +91(011) 23276843-44, Fax: +91(011) 23276863
e-mail: kapoor@anebooks.com, Website: www.anebooks.com

Branch Office:

- Avantika Niwas, 1st Floor, 19 Doraiswamy Road, T. Nagar,
  Chennai - 600 017, Tel.: +91(044) 28141554, 28141209
  e-mail: anebookschennai@gmail.com, rathinam@anebooks.com

ISBN : 978-81-80522-37-6

Printed at R.K. Offset Process, New Delhi

Preface

When all of us were associated with Fortune Institute of International Business in New Delhi the family as a whole hold a series of brain storming sessions to identify areas in which organisations will have to reorient themselves to successfully bring about a transition from a controlled to open economy in India. We believe that the problems of transition need to be recognised by management and teachers alike. In this study attention was extended to family managed businesses, multinationals and public sector enterprises.

This book concerns what may best be described as sociology of organisations. We have studied management styles of family managed businesses, multinationals and public sector enterprises and the problems of adjustment of employees to new requirements. Based on our data we have suggested action plans for the management to meet the requirements of the emerging situation in business. The sample includes fourteen chief executives drawn from all three categories. These companies responded to our request for in-depth interviews and in some cases with their immediate subordinates. In three companies we interviewed employees as well to understand the problems of adjustment within the organisation. We have withheld the name of companies on their request, except in two cases who had no objection to using their names.

The Study was confined to Delhi and it's surrounding areas and was partially funded by Fortune Institute of International Business. We are grateful to the Institute for the support.

Ishwar Dayal
Mirza S. Saiyadain
Deepak Dogra
Kewal Sony
Poornima Gupta
Lubna Nafees

Contents

	Preface	*v*
1.	The Newer Demands on Organisations	1-16
2.	The Nature of the Study and the Sample	17-20
3.	The Management Style in Family Businesses	21-38
4.	Managing Styles of Multinationals	39-48
5.	The Management Styles in Public Sector Enterprises	49-62
6.	Job Satisfaction and Organisational Culture	63-78
7.	Preparing for New Challenges	79-106
8.	Survey of Literature	107-116
	References	117-124
	Case Studies	125-150
	• *Case Study* - I : Kamla Dials & Devices Ltd.	127-140
	• *Case Study* - II : Atlas Cycles	141-150
	Index	151-156

Chapter 1

The Newer Demands on Organisations

The management practices in India developed during the sixty years of controlled economy. For long periods the country faced shortages of goods resulting in predominantly a sellers market. With no competitive pressures, the organisations did not have a compelling need for continuing concern for product development, innovation, quality of product, cost, technology upgradation and such aspects of management. The shift to the open market situation and global competition requires vastly pressing attention to developing organisational and managerial practices. These considerations would require considerable reorientation of management systems and practices in almost all functions including the way of looking at business by all levels of management hierarchy, including the top. Organisations would have to give special attention to efficiency, productivity, innovation, creativity and such considerations. These attributes would invite special attention to behvaioural and cultural issues both in the market place and employees at the work place. The teaching of management would have to undertake research to understand fully the nature of changes required and possible action plan to bring about the transition. The present report based on field interviews is one such exercise. Series of other reports that will follow in due course had to be geared to understanding the issues involved in transition by organisations in India from a stable to a volatile and dynamic market situation. The decision to open market access will attract companies from abroad with established brand image, advanced technology and resources at their command. These would require some urgency for developing competitive strength in Indian organisations. Failure to do so could reduce market acceptance and perhaps, in many cases, lead to demise of business. Hence, the authors believe that besides the problems associated with competition in the market place, a whole range of issues relating to globalisation need attention.

The Institute's first thrust area was to take up people related issues such as dynamics of cross-cultural relations, management of diversity and related organisational considerations. Success of technological, organisational and managerial considerations in fact rests on a positive response of concerned people. Change in ways of thinking, new orientation and desire to cooperate and absorb developments by individuals and groups is the key to organisational effectiveness. The present report concerns itself with the processes of adaptation, involvement and identification to the organisation and the work. These are essential for people to respond to changing demands.

The book relates to business groups which constitute the largest category in business: the family managed, the multinationals and the public sector enterprises. We realize that there are marked differences between these categories of organisations as also within each category. However, in each category a very large number fall into a pattern which characterise their management styles and work methods. We have taken this overall pattern in each case to understand the problem areas within the management system and the possible action choices required for growth, and indeed long term survival of their business.

Another reason for taking up these three categories of enterprises is the role that each has played in the past and a continuing role that they are likely to play in the years to come. At the same time it is necessary to recognize that the survival of a large number of them will depend upon their ability and determination to reorient themselves for the challenges in the emerging environment. This consideration applies specially to family managed businesses, multinationals and public sector enterprises. The multinationals would also have to recognize the need for integrating their approaches with the psycho-social factors that we believe will require attention. This book analyses the nature of problem areas in respect to the styles of managing by decision makers and a possible approach to move ahead. The data for this study is based on the interviews carried out by the authors, and to some extent, their consulting experiences.

The organisations in the West have always been open to competition. In post World War-II scenario, the competition became sharper on account of developments in technology and sciences. New applications of knowledge in products, operations and demand patterns caused organisations to change in the way of carrying out their businesses. In this process organisations that failed to adjust to constantly changing demands of markets fell by the way side. Over time the competition became more intense and they felt pressures to expand their markets globally.

Many developing countries had to open their boundaries for internal reasons of low growth or stagnation in their economies. The resulting globalisation of business have brought pressures to reorient their business organisations as the West was obliged to do earlier. The developing countries have an additional consideration. The business organisations have operated for more than sixty years in centrally controlled and primarily non-competitive market environment. The management systems and the ways of doing business in turn have also become responsive to the then prevailing business conditions, except in high technology businesses such as information technology, bio-technology, etc. which have emerged in more recent years. As observed over the years the strength of the business community in India and that of Indians in general is their entrepreneurship. However, there is difference between an entrepreneurial and a managerial role and this difference should be recognized. This aspect is discussed further in the book. A number of organisations have reoriented themselves but according to available data there are many who have yet to do so. Besides major reorganisation of the system, this exercise has to involve the styles of managing business at the top levels and the mental set of the employees. The management systems evolved in the West have emerged out of their own socio-cultural background. In reorienting our business organisations we would have to be guided by our own cultural ethos because response of people for developing an environment of working together, the emotional response is essential for involvement in what they do. In competitive environment responsibility for results has to be widely shared. This is likely to come when management systems are consistent with the culture and tradition in which a large number of people have grown. The Japanese have adapted the management concepts to harmonise with their cultural orientation. The Chinese and the Koreans have also done so. The Indian organisations need to reorient their management systems to harmonise with the native culture and tradition. This books is concerned with identifying the core elements of the Indian societal ethos and management systems and practices that would be consistent with the Indian environment. The discussion elaborates the direction that could lead to the commitment of employees to work and the organisation.

Organisations would have to employ technology and use developments in science to develop competitive products, improve procedures and processes. The optimum use of these developments would depend on the willingness of employees to absorb and internalize these developments. At the core of all considerations of development is the man and his inner urge to cooperate or distance himself from the situation. His coping strategies in respect to changing requirements rest with his involvement or identification with his work and the organisation to which he belongs. This book primarily reflects on the nature of organisational practices in each category of organisations that will bring about the employee's attachment and cooperation or distance him from what he is required to do. The managerial action plans and strategies would have to be inevitably linked to the cultural moorings of the population. The internationally noted psychoanalyst Sudhir Kakar and Kathariana Kakar comment,

"The cultural part of our personal identity, modern neuroscience tells us, is wired into our brain. The culture in which an infant grows up constitutes the software of the brain, much of which is already in place by the end of childhood". Kakars further quote neurologist and philosopher Gerhard Roth who observes, "Irrespective of its genetic endowment, a human baby growing up in Africa, Europe or Japan will become an African, an European or a Japanese. And once someone has grown up in a particular culture and let us say, is twenty years old, he will never acquire a full understanding of other cultures since the brain has passed through the narrow bottleneck of culturalisation". (Kakar and Kakar, 2007, p.2). The involvement of individuals is related to the social environment at work which is familiar to him and is ingrained in his psyche. This view is widely shared by many social scientists. In a global setting adjustment and involvement of people in the organisation and to the environment is essential and this is possible only when the management is able to create a will to cooperate on the part of employees and the customers. We believe that in this direction the questions that this book has raised and discussed will be useful for managers and students.

Nature of Demand on Organisations

What is the nature of demands that globalisation and competitive market environment would make on an organisation?

Based on our in-depth interviews, we have discussed in separate chapters the styles of managing family managed, multinationals and public sector organisations and broadly suggested the kind of changes that would be necessary in each case for developing the organisation's capability to compete globally. In this chapter we have outlined the capabilities required to handle certain key areas of business and later in chapter seven we have put all the pieces together to suggest a possible approach to adapt organisations to deal with the imperatives of the emerging business environment.

Market Related Issues

The product features, the quality and price of product would have greater appeal to a large number of customers than the established standing of the company. Until recently products introduced and marketed by certain companies were accepted without hesitation. Such a situation is unlikely to prevail in the future. This change has taken place in US & Europe also. Apart from the marketing strategies, organisations would have to develop design expertise and new applications of their product range for maintaining a stable client base and to hold their competitive position. The life-cycle of products will continuously become shorter and shorter. One organisation in durable product range mentioned to us that it took them two years of research to develop a new device to improve efficiency of the cooling chamber but they can only expect about six months of lead start in the market because competitors will perhaps bring out similar or improved devices. Changes in models would have to be planned well in advance and in many cases the range would have to be market or customer segment specific.

Rapid Developments in science and technology bring out new materials and new applications. The market intelligence system in ogranisations would have to keep a tab on relevant developments that concern their products. Some organisations are known to have given scholarships for Ph.D studies in scientific institutions to know what kind of researches are being undertaken by scientists and their relevance for their companies.

The technology has assumed an important role in distribution, promotion and warehousing of goods and services. The IT expertise has critical contribution to make in developing systems and continuously updating them. In brief, in all market related operations the situation is highly dynamic and people concerned have to be constantly aware of the factors that influence their product, cost, quality and be aware of customer preferences. No successful marketing functionary can work alone, he has to work together with people within the organisation and the markets outside the organisation. Taking any situation for granted can be fatal to business irrespective of the size of the organisation.

In brief the marketing function in the competitive environment would change in many significant ways. The most important changes are identified below:

i. Marketing is no longer a departmental function. The entire organisation has to become sensitive to customer and markets– the product development, quality and cost of production, production planning to respond to market changes, pricing to compete with competitors, HR initiative to make employees become sensitive to changes and so on. All these functionaries would have to have a feel for the market conditions.

ii. A strong market intelligence system to remain one step ahead of the competitors, and be prepared for developments that would affect business.

iii. Need for building customer profile and maintain continuing contacts with major customers, dealers, stockists and any other intermediatory groups. Life cycle of products being short, the company has to be able to feel the pulse of the market.

iv. Expertise and organisational mechanism would have to be developed to review marketing and sales strategies involving inter-functional teams.

v. All functional departments in companies which have highly competitive product groups would have to provide and be geared to support the marketing efforts. In this sense every function has to relate to the company's assessment of what the customer and the market requires. For example if the cost competitive product is required by the market, the production has to develop technological systems and controls that could result in the desired level of cost. Other functions likewise have to support the market activities of the company (Verma, 2007).

These are some of the major approaches that companies have had to consider. There would be some other considerations that apply to specific product groups which the concerned organisations would have to examine.

Organisation Related Issues

Speed and sharing of information about operations widely within the organisation would be necessary for people to develop sensitivity to the market. Several organisations have continuing practice to send their employees to spend one day in a week or a month to visit markets. This helps all employees to become sensitive to customers and markets. This is a regular practice in LG Electronics, Hindustan Lever and many other organisations abroad and also in India. National Thermal Power Corporation, a public sector enterprise documents best operating practices for use of all their spread out units with the objective that other units adapt them in their own context.

Many organisations in US and Europe have also developed what has come to be known as knowledge management. Briefly, this exercise consists of obtaining data and information from all sources outside the organisation and developments in related areas to benefit operations within the organisation. The exercise is also necessary for awareness of the developments, the events all over the globe so as to create openness and sensitivity of managers to the environment. Knowledge beyond one's organsational boundaries, world view of socio-political and economic issues could help in updating policy and perspectives. Many organisations have off-site brain storming sessions to generate new ideas.

Most Organisations in India have to develop strong data base to keep abreast of developments and devise systems to analyse them for relevance to their own situation.

Another concern has to do with costs of management. This exercise in most organisations is not confined to inventory control or waste reduction alone but invariably requires totally new perspectives of doing work. Some examples will illustrate this point. When Louis V. Gerstner Jr. came to IBM as CEO which had lost its primacy in business to other companies, the choice was to either revive it or face further decline. The new CEO found that the organisation suffered from a tall hierarchy one-over-one arrangement of positions. When he asked anyone question on the progress of a project he was told that he would find out although he had the responsibility for the project. The practice was that the person concerned merely distributed work to a large number of people and he as in-charge merely "supervised" the project. As in a bureaucracy, a large number of positions were created down the line which did not do anything by themselves except supervise the work of others. The new CEO collapsed the levels and each person was given direct operating responsibility. A large number of people were sent out to explore field operations where contact with customers and information about their preferences was necessary. The cost management and efficiency in many organisations in India require comprehensive exercise of re-engineering systems of work and processes. The measures of the kind mentioned in IBM are important for speedy and necessary communication.

The rearrangement of work system and assigning clearly defined responsibility for results strengthens the organisation's capability to bring customer consciousness and involvement in the position that each person holds. The system of periodic review of practices and polices would become necessary to keep the organisation dynamic.

The R&D would have to perform a more crucial role than it had done so far in most organisations. Familiarity with technology and up-gradation of technology would be necessary to hold quality and price of the product.

As organisations integrate with world economy they would have to develop capability for managing diversity, cross cultural issues and consensus building skills. Lack of competence in these aspects of business could hinder progress. In many oranisations handling differences on a day to day basis diverts attention of managers from customer and market to fire-fighting on operating issues. The competence in these aspects of business does not develop through lectures and seminars but the experience of working together. Varma in his book about LG Electronics relates an interesting experience from early years of LG's life in India. He went to the Korean Chief Executive with the problem that Korean and Indian staff were indulging in finding faults with one another and that the problem was spreading. He suggested that they should organise series of discussion groups to bring about better understanding among them. The CEO said that the discussion groups would not solve the problem: when they jointly work on problems a better understanding would develop. Verma said that this approach did solve the problem without discussing such matters in seminars. (Verma, 2007). Most organisations in India have to consciously develop understanding of dealing with cross-cultural issues and diversity, and develop positive ways to handle them. The social scientists have developed many ways to develop positive approaches in dealing with differences. However, not many organisations in India have taken advantage to develop these skills.

Organisations would have to undertake structural changes to respond to the demands of the business and bring about behavioural adjustments. The adaptability to changes at all levels of the ogranisation is essential for success (Grestner, 2002).

Technology

In non-competitive situation and in assured market conditions, quality and cost of product in most organisations did not receive much attention. Besides the technology expansion in the world occurred in more recent year. The technology development in earlier periods was incremental.

In India serious concern for technology perhaps goes back to mid eighties. India has lost its primacy in many industries such as textile, some agriculture products, etc. because China, Japan, Malaysia had earlier installed superior technology. No country can possibly compete globally unless the operating systems are able to compete in cost, quality, speedy delivery system and service. Outlook of most employees in India is not geared to technology.

In many organisations technological change has not served the intended purpose. Most cases of failure are ascribable to inadequate preparation of people and support systems to use technology. In many cases there is little awareness on the part of management to deal with anxieties of individuals about loss of jobs and lack of confidence to learn new skills. In some cases the new system breaks up the established social groups within the work place. Such unconscious feelings brings out negative reactions to change. The literature on technological change provides many accounts of success and failure in organisations. Technological change requires much more than installing modern machinery. It requires simultaneous changes in respect to operating systems, management policies and practices and readiness of employees to learn new skills.

Human Side of Business

The ogranisations would need at least three outcomes of the human organisation:

i. Responsibility for results and involvement in work
ii. Cooperation and a spirit of working together
iii. Creativity

These characteristics exist within most human beings. But they have to be brought out. The relevant issue is what should organisations do to bring out these features among people and how should they be sustained. The competitive strength of the ogranisation would depend upon how these features develop among people.

It is a common observation that an individual does well in one situation and does poorly in another. One chief executive mentioned after a prolonged period of strike in his factory that union members had organised the strike remarkably well. However, at work if they showed less than half of the capability that they showed in organising strike and keeping nearly 15,000 employees away from the factory without salary for about six months, the company could do wonders in the market place. The people at work showed not even a fraction of this capability. An in-depth study of chronic absentees in a factory revealed that most of them remained absent to do highly skilled jobs elsewhere because they enjoyed that work (Vaid, 1969). They often remained absent to engage in occasional assignments elsewhere. Goethe said "Treat people as if they were what they ought to be and you help them to become what they are capable of being'.

Experience of many organisations and research data bring out the following considerations relating to human organisation:

i. Selection of individuals with potential is important but their compatability would not reflect in the job without organisational and management practices consciously aimed at developing this potential.

ii. People get involved in the job when they derive pleasure from what they are doing. When this happens they are likely to be creative and assume responsibility for results. Rabindranath Tagore in one of his writings wondered why cannot we make jobs as pleasurable as game.

iii. involvement in work is a far greater motivator than financial incentives (Brown, 1960).

iv. In most cases capabilities of people lie dormant unless the environment brings it out. The limits of capabilities in individuals are often stretchable.

v. Under normal conditions many individuals often are not conscious of their capability to learn but with sympathetic support and help they can bring these out. (Wiedman, 1955).

Some of the experiences, based on the assumptions made above are discussed in the concluding chapter.

In brief, we have outlined some special considerations that are necessary to successfully operate in the emerging economic and business environment. The analysis in the following chapters of the family managed businesses, multinationals and public sector enterprises are based on the premise that they have to develop organisational and managerial capabilities to effectively respond to such requirements for their own growth and indeed survival. Our suggestions for modification in managerial style in each case are also based on the organisational requirements as outlined here. Chapter-7 pulls the data from the earlier chapters and outlines approaches to prepare an organisation for developing a climate of working together.

It may also be necessary to repeat that there are vast differences within each category of organisations. Our discussion takes into consideration e.g. a "typical" organisation, not the one's that have already taken steps to anticipate and deal with the emerging demands.

Chapter 2

The Nature of the Study and the Sample

We have drawn our sample for the study from fourteen ourganisations. The sample includes five family managed organisations in a variety of product groups. Two of these are in engineering "low-technology" areas, two others in consumer electronics and one in financial services.

The multinational companies are from Japan, Korea, United States, United Kingdom, Netherlands and Germany. Of these companies, two from the United Kingdom, one each from Japan and Netherlands have been in the country for more than 25 years. The reason for including in the sample companies with around 10 years in India and those with more than 25 years standing is to see if their managing styles are influenced by longer years in the country. The fourteenth organisation is an association of employers which handles members from different background and orientation. In all the fourteen organisations the research team has interviewed in depth the Chief Executives and in some cases managers reporting to them. The sample from public enterprises is drawn from heavy engineering, electronics, process industries and service organisations.

We have also interviewed employees in three organisation; one from a family managed company, another from a multinational and a third from a high tech organisaton. The purpose of taking up a sample of employees at operating levels is to understand if the process of adjustment by employees in these companies is different from that of the manager.

In the interviews our concerns were threefold:

i. Are there any characteristic ways of managing the three types of business organisations.
ii. Are there differences in the styles of managing companies by chief executives coming from different cultural orientation.
iii. What characterises the management styles in family managed business organisations in high-tech compared to the one in traditional technology.

Deriving from the data obtained in the interviews, we have discussed the nature of problem areas that family managed, multinationals and public enterprises will face as the Indian economy becomes more competitive. Further, based on this analysis, what changes each would have to make to adjust to the emerging demands.

The interviews with chief executives and managers were open ended. However a guideline was available for the areas to be covered in the interviews. The employees were interviewed on the basis of a structured questionnaire. We had planned to interview employees in all companies in the sample but this could not be done due to paucity of time and research support funds.

The relevance of the study is that new demands would be made on existing organisations in a competitive situation. The organisations would have to evolve practices for speedy decision making, constant review of product-range in the changing market environment, aggressive approaches in strategy formulation and environment that can promote innovation at policy and operating levels. At present such conditions prevail in limited number of organisations. Operating in a somewhat stable and relatively non-competitive environment, the organisations have been successful with centralised system of decision making, a tall hierarchy and somewhat un-urgent responses to business and organisational issues. During the last few years some organisations have undertaken measures to cope with emerging demands but most systematic studies, including ours, show that many organisations in the country would have to make some fundamental changes in approach to maintain their market standing.

Most multinationals have a different style of management but need orientation in integrating their approach with the culture and tradition of the wider society in which they operate. A majority of public sector enterprises are modeled after Government and function in the mould of a bureaucracy. The system is driven by top levels of the hierarchy and the orientation of the CEO influences critically its functioning style.

Broadly characteristics of the situation in three types of organisations suggests that

i. having grown in a protective environment most Indian organisations have developed organisational and management systems that are not entirely responsive to the emerging competitive environment

ii. the multinationals from abroad bring their own styles of working, systems and practices which in some ways do not harmonise with the Indian societal patterns of behaviour. There is dichotomy between the wider society and the organisational cultures. The employees who come from highly structured traditional norms of behaviour live two lives; one at home and another in the company. This situation could induce mental health problems among some employees. Such a dichotomy could also encourage such employees to leave when wage levels in national organisations reach comparable levels to that of multinationals. If this situation prevails the companies will face problems of high employee turnover.

iii. The public sector enterprises follow a bureaucratic functional model with central authority resting with higher levels of management. An emerging competitive environment has already imposed strains at operating and strategy levels and many of them are facing challenges in the market place. This situation is likely to become more acute in the emerging competitive environment. Perhaps only strong technology based organisations would continue to hold their position due to their product or service.

The management practices in organisations set up by techno-managers who are in most cases entrepreneurs have evolved a pattern which is somewhere in between the family managed and the multinationals. The impact of these practices on employees and the organisation is different. It is likely that they may face problems as the technology develops and makes specific demands for rapid changes in operating practices. The book highlights some of these problem areas.

Chapter 3

The Management Style in Family Businesses

The study included four successful and growth-oriented family managed organisations operating in different product groups. Two companies managed by a family were traditional low-technology oriented manufacturing companies and moving on to specialised retail business. The third family managed company was in entertainment consumer durable product category operating in a vastly competitive field and the fourth company managed by family was in financial sector. We had separate semi-structured interviews with workers in these organisations to understand how they responded to the work environment of these companies.

Characteristics of Family Managed Businesses

The origin of family business lies in entrepreneurship of a core individual. In most cases the individual received support from the members of the family in the joint family system which have strong affiliative bonds. There is a stereotype in the minds of most individuals about family businesses. We found that while there are many common features in the style of management in family managed businesses, there are also marked differences among them. The common features of family businesses are the following:-

i. They value loyalty and reposed considerable faith in their trusted people. In low technology based organisations the family members manage through individuals or a select group who perform a link or filtering process. They are the eyes and ears of the family members. They provide the feedback to the CEO and receive instructions from him. Such persons become almost like family members and socially interact with the family. Invariably they attend social and religious functions in the household. In this pattern they are more than an employee. All other managers and employees recognise this special position and relate to them as special functionaries referred to here as supra-managers. Normally other employees do not have direct access to CEO except when they are called. In a typical low-technology based organisation the supra-managers also function through people who are loyal to them. Such people function as intermediaries between the supra-managers and the employees. They function as their "eyes and ears" and give them the feedback about whatever happens at the work level. As a result such employees expect and receive rewards for being loyal, and not necessarily on considerations of merit or performance. In this manner the social organisation rests primarily on relationships among people holding linking positions. However, the loyalty-based managerial style also creates in-groups and out-groups, i.e. people who are close to the supra-managers and those who are not. Invariably in this system individuals who are considered as "troublesome" are either pushed sideways or 'accommodated'. People are mostly seen as individuals and handled in that way. In case trade unions are formed in such organisations, the relations with the leaders is invariably based on accommodation.

ii. Family members are seen as father-figures in organisations where employees are fairly satisfied with conditions of work and the management is seen to be benevolent. In one organisation the employees approached the CEO (family member) to advise them about what they should do in case of prolonged differences between managers and employees. The CEO was requested to be arbiter in the situation. However, these situations prevail in established organisations which have a majority of employees with long service, say 15 years and above. Some younger people even in established organisations want to know their rights and privileges. There is evidence of shift from family–like relationships to a more formal basis.

iii. Introduction of new technology is a rare occurrence partly because the established relationships are disturbed. In most cases the family members are fairly satisfied with incremental returns. In last twenty years or so many of these industries have shown decline.

iv. Invariably the second or third generation with more than one grown-up member of the family, the businesses or functions are divided. In our sample, the businesses were legally divided because the family members were unable to agree on growth related issues on many operating matters. The business experienced decline till the family decided to divide the business on agreed basis.

v. Most of the largest family-managed business houses of 1950s have been split among family members by 1980s. For example the family business groups such as Mafatlals, Birla, Bajaj, Kasturbhai, Sarabhai, DCM and many others are split by now.

vi. All entrepreneurial decisions are generally taken by the family without formal consultation with people within the organisations.

Family Managed Organisations having Technology Base

The family managed companies which have technology base have also strong belief in loyalty but they have somewhat more structured arrangement. There are designated positions and in most operating matters activity is carried out through these positions. However the feedback to CEO is regular in frequent face-to-face discussions with operating head. The contact of CEO with the managers and other employees is mainly when they are summoned. The targets of performance are set by CEO who keeps a closer watch over sales and finances. At times CEO supervises these functions direct. New products, development and growth, diversification and such matters are more likely to be initiated by CEO than the people within the organisation. Invariably the ideas for development come from the CEO's business contacts or his observations of things during trips abroad. In one company a trusted employee was given a roaming responsibility to visit organisations and universities, etc. in India and abroad to seek out developments. On return he gave detailed report on what he observed and had discussed with people during his visit, especially the contacts that he developed with knowledgeable people. Occasionally in some organisations certain demands are made or suggestions come from senior people, specially those who form the in-group of the CEO. The requests for changes in machinery or changes in the manufacturing processes come from the operating managers. In some cases budgets are prepared but they are rarely used for purposes of control.

Business Consideration

Among the growth oriented and technology based industry there is distinct realisation that "professionalising" management is necessary. However the concept of "professionalising" appears to be vague in most cases. In some cases it amounts to recruiting qualified people from recognised technical and management schools. In principle the policy making function is separated from executive functions. However, in an on-going situation the clear demarcation of the two is operationally difficult. To the extent the final decision making role lies with a family member as perceived by employees, the top level dichotomy is difficult to avoid. What's more, policy making requires 'realistic' understanding of the operational issues and the CEO (family member) relies largely on interpretation of someone who provides information or data on various operating matters to him or her. It is also common in most organisations that employees even at senior level positions do not give their opinions and provide data that they feel the boss wants. The data feedback in most Indian organisations is rarely open, much less in family businesses.

Some ways of working in the enterprise encourages such behaviour, and often induces "professionals" to leave or follow the 'norms' of the enterprise. One highly regarded officer in HRD function mentioned that he had developed in consultation with consultants, a battery of tests for selection and laid down a procedure which was endorsed by the CEO who was a family member. But from time to time he received a slip from the CEO to appoint such and such person in a position disregarding the procedure he had approved. The Manager said this kind of over-riding orders were received in a number of situations. After a while the individual concerned decided to leave the company. In another company a systems manager with very high remuneration was appointed. He said that the job described to him at the interview was most attractive and one that he was looking for. After six months he decided to leave the job because in spite of best efforts he could see the CEO (a family member) only once for a few minutes and no one else would give him any directions about the company. He said he did not want to sit idle day after day waiting for an appointment with the CEO. These are not isolated instances but repeated in many companies. Such events contribute to norm-setting in the organisation.

In yet another family-managed organisation the CEO, a family head prided in public that his companies do not entertain any favours to Government employees for the clearances or licences that they obtain from concerned people. However, senior managers in our interactions with them mentioned that they handle these matters and satisfy the concerned people and do not tell this to the CEO because he prides in "getting things done" without gratification. We book these expenses under different expenditure heads for the Head Office. The examples given here are not related to family businesses alone but the same patterns are observed in many organisations in the country.

The family businesses are characterised by two additional aspects. Because employees perceive, and believe, in the fact that top position would always be occupied by a family member, more ambitious and initiative-prone managers leave the job and seek their destiny where they can reach the top of the hierarchy. The research team members in their consulting and research have observed this pattern repeatedly. The managers who stay back rarely provide unfavourable data, or share their apprehensions with their seniors, much less with a family member. Another common occurrence is that as the family grows (specially second or third generation) the growing family size and ambitions of individual members compel break-up of the business. In a competitive environment the strength of the business lies in constant infusion of technology and development and these tasks need financial support which smaller units resulting from division of business may not be able to provide.

The family is a basic unit with its own norms of behaviour and individuals in it imbibe at least unconsciously, its values. The family environment in most families follow a tradition of respect for elders, hierarchy and a strong sense of belonging to the family. Nigel Nicholson who teaches family-owned business management in London Business School said in an interview that "the Indian family is blessed because of the value system it inculcates" (Nicholson, 2007). The business operationally follow the norms of the family, Some family members, for example, mentioned that when some employees of the business organisation came to visit them at the university abroad where they were students, they stood up in their presence or touched their feet, and inspite of attempts on their part to establish relationships on a different basis, the employees continued to relate as if they were the benefactors.

Many of the younger generation aspire to enter other diversified business segments and manage them independently on their own. Some of the younger members in the family mentioned that they get recognition and social status by being in a position to oblige and bestow favours on others. They believe that unlike earlier years they can gain social recognition as a CEO and not necessarily as a member of a family. Many want authority and power and independence to follow their own will. They need an independent identity. As families grow in size, members of second and third generation cannot be easily absorbed in family businesses.

On the part of elders in the family, the care and acceptance is lacking that had characterized their role for harmonising the family and the business in the past. We observed that in some cases the younger people accepted and respected the elders in the family but found them less acceptable as business leaders. They feel that such matters can rarely be discussed in the family environment but these unexpressed feelings adversely influence the conduct of business. In one family where we were able to attend discussion on a business problem by members of the family, the concerns that many members had earlier mentioned in separate discussions with us were not openly brought out.

In another family situation the individual members in private conversation were critical of some other members for their lack of interest and application in business but in meetings such feelings were not shared. Such feelings are suppressed and it is more than likely that the unresolved feelings strain decision processes in the organisation. Decision making is delayed. The hidden agenda in relationships causes strain at work.

Advantages of Family Management

The family as a unit provide many advantages for business. These are briefly mentioned here.

i. On account of family interest the entrepreneurial leadership is available to the organisation. The entrepreneurial decisions are taken quickly and acted upon. The industrial capabilities in the country have indeed been developed, besides the public sector, by family entrepreneurship.

ii. There are a number of employees owning loyalty to the CEO. The plans and instructions are made without loss of time and implemented. In this manner there is cohesiveness in approach at the top level of the organisation. Study by Katrinoli and Colleagues (2006) reports that values in the organisation were congruent with family values and ensured their continuance from one generation to another. This was facilitated by the family members absorbing the values in the process of growing up and these values are reflected in business as well.

iii. The CEO has personal stake in the results of the enterprise and this provides a motive for his involvement in the conduct of business. Sir Anthony Banford who has built up a highly successful company called Banford Excavators known as JCB, is the largest manufacturer of construction equipment in the united Kingdom. They export 75% of the product to 140 countries. Sir Anthony mentioned in an interview that because of family ownership they are not terribly concerned about annual budgets and profits: rather they are able to take at least a five year perspective in terms of performance and growths. This helps the company grow in a sound manner.

iv. Being a joint family the financial resources are pooled and available for investment in business. In this respect there is small danger of any takeover bid of business by outsiders. After a bid to take over Escorts and DCM by a UK based company headed by Swaraj Paul the families have made deliberate attempt to increase the family's share holding from around 10-11% to at least 25%. The companies concerned were able to ward-off the bid with the support of the representative directors of financial institutions.

v. There is consistency in the management approaches. This provides stability to the company and the employees.

Disadvantages of the Family Type Management

The dependence proneness of employees as a characteristic of individuals in India is further reinforced in the managerial style in the organsiation. They look upto management for succor in every respect. They take their job in a primarily mechanical way i.e., do what is assigned. Any effort to go beyond the limited boundary is rare, resulting in separation of self from work. The reinforcement of dependence proneness and the style of working rarely generates involvement and urge to innovate. Routinisation of organisational tasks has two other consequences. First, employees become so used to the routine that they find adjustment to new or evolving situations difficult. Second, employees relate on one-to-one superior–subordinate and hierarchical relations where team working is rarely possible.

The Problem Areas

The family managed businesses are increasingly concerned about the pattern of family relationships besides the changing demands of business. They have to conceptualise and develop a system to meet the aspirations of increasing numbers of family members and at the same time retain employees who seek recognition. As many writers have pointed out that assured and automatic succession, now prevailing in family owned businesses, could impair the organisation. The succession is assumed both at the family and the organisation levels. In a sense this pattern has become a tradition in family managed businesses and any change in this would be hard to bring about. At present the alternative route is found in terms of dividing the assets of the company among the aspirants. This practice has long term implications on growth at least for most companies which are not sustainable as independent units. This point has also been discussed earlies in the chapter.

In the emerging environment of business, the existing pattern of work environment in the family managed organisations, have serious limitations. In the controlled market environment the cost, quality, efficiency, innovation etc., had limited impact on the market performance of the organisation where as in the emerging competitive environment, these aspects of work are critical for the survival of a business. In addition, the development and innovative capacity of the organsiation will depend on the company's capacity to provide growth opportunities for talented persons. Hence the long term survival of family managed organisations would depend on significant changes in the styles of management. Some changes in the basic patterns or styles of management for long term survival are identified below:-

i. The supra-manager system would have to be replaced by people who hold organisational positions. CEO would always have to rely on other people to carry out managerial and operational work. The difference is that these position holders would have to be themselves responsible for results, not the functionaries who provide intermediary links as supra-managers invariably do. This system would require formalisation of positions, authority, identification of result areas and an effective review system.

ii. The growth and development has to become a deliberate exercise in the strategic planning system. These considerations are at times sacrificed in the interest of the family. In one conglomerate we observed that even major investment decisions were taken to suit the convenience of certain family members without a project report or detailed study of the market feasibility.

   In another large multi-unit company we found that all investment decisions yielded in losses for the company but the Board never questioned the family why such decisions were taken without a study.

iii. The work organisation would need serious review to determine how employees can be involved in work and be responsible for results. It is the experience of researchers that most organisations needed special attention to re-design and reengineer the work processes of jobs in manufacturing as well as in offices.

iv. These changes would require considerable effort in reorienting employees at all levels and continuous training programmes.

v. The reorientation of work practices and attitudes of employees towards work and relationships in the organisation is possible only when the process begins at the top levels of management. In almost all cases the individual and his family members will have to reorient themselves.

vi. The family relationships and business affairs are often mixed and the decision taken affect both.

vii. As children in the second and third generation grow, the struggle to control business grows and this phenomenon influences both family relationships and business performance. In our sample also this phenomena had occurred, as the business began to show marked signs of decline, the families decided to split with the help of mutually accepted professional groups. In yet another organisation the professional managers were given the operating management i.e. the day to day working, and the family confined itself to policy issues, although they sat in the same building. However the experience suggests that this arrangement has limitations. As the company grows in size, the strains in this arrangement are likely to create uncertainties in the minds of operating managers. Some organisations in the West have found a solution for family managed companies by confining their activities to strategic decisions, leaving total management of the enterprise to professional managers.

Some Experiences of Coping

The family managed businesses have tried several models to deal with business requirements. Some typical models are mentioned here-

i. The CEO and the head of the family took steps to initiate his sons to learn the business from grassroots. For example Sir Shri Ram assigned his sons to work in the DCM mills to acquire first-hand experience of the various textile departments. In more recent months, Ranbaxy promoted a manager to the top position and the owner's son worked in the business to gain experience. However the son automatically took over the position when the executive retired.

ii. Another approach is provided by Eicher Tractors. The Chief Executive removed himself from the position and appointed another person to head the business. He set-up an advisory group consisting of eminent people including himself to review the overall company performance from time to time. This committee had no executive responsibility.

iii. A third approach is found in some organisations in USA and Europe. No family member has executive role in the company and the family maintains only financial interest. In some cases the family members constitute a Board which approve budgets and growth plans of the company. The plans for diversification, expansion or major investments are approved in pre-planned meetings of this Board. The family members depend on the income from their investment in the company but follow their respective interests individually.

One difficulty in this arrangement is that in most established companies in India the family holdings are small, although in most high technology companies the family holding is substantial.

iv. A fourth approach which is rare, is that younger people have taken up appointments elsewhere while retaining financial interest in the company. This strategy is employed more for training in a variety of different organisations while other members of the family manage the business. On return the younger members invariably assume the CEO position.

We believe that a direction for sustained well-being is provided by some of the technology based companies, especially those concerned with Information Technology (IT). such as Wipro, Infosys, and some others. The family owners hold substantial financial interest in the company but employ 'professional' managers to manage the company. The select group works in executive position for some years and absorb the culture and tradition of the company. The members of the select group function in key positions and in reasonable time the family members hand over total operations to them. They ensure that such persons have absorbed the value systems and culture of the organisation. This is important because the company's continuity and transition should be non-threatening to employees and customers. In some companies a family member holds the position of chairman of the Board but does not function as a proprietor. There is every indication that anyone from the company can assume top level position depending upon his performance. If a family member joins the company he has to earn his position by his performance. These companies appoint Board members who have qualifications to provide help and function as Directors, in line with the indications of the regulations in the company law. The family owned and managed companies in the West have followed this approach.

Nigel Nicholson suggests that families should not have a rigid rule about who should be the successor to head the organisation. He maintains that the family should not exit from the business because the family name gives the business market standing and the company is able to take long term view of business (Nicholson, 2006). It is possible that Nicholson's conclusions are based on the data of migrant families from Asian and African countries such as Uganda and Kenya because they would be operating in an alien environment where ethnic groups have strong social bonds. These bonds are induced partly by the inner feeling of aliens to protect their identity. In this environment the phenomenon of split in the family led by ambition and social recognition is less important than maintaining viability of business. In the environment of one's own country the second and third generation family members have powerful motive to acquire and hold positions of authority and power. In most cases if the split does not occur the business decisions are invariably delayed. Vested interests among family members adversely affect the decision making process. We observed this in our study of Atlas Cycle and Kamla Dials as shown in the annexures of this book. Nusli Wadia suggests that after first five years, the family should leave the business to professional management. We presume that the importance of this suggestion is that beyond the stage of critical entrepreneurial action, the management should rest with professional managers.

Most writers abroad and successful practitioners such as Sir Anthony Banford suggest that succession should not be assured.

He also emphasised that the family instills important values among their children such as hard work and delegation which are critical for the success of an enterprise. He further clarified that 'delegation means having faith in people, an aspect not very uncommon among many families (this refers to UK situation) and have long term vision in all financial matters' (McCuttoch, 2006). Two of the three sons of Sir Banford are engaged in professions of their own choosing and the third after completing his studies, is contemplating taking up a marketing position in the family business. This pattern is repeated in many family managed organisations in the UK.

The family managed businesses have certain distinct advantage of experience, continuity of management approaches and a combination of caution and risk taking. However, family managed businesses in most developing countries have to take some models from the West to survive in a competitive environment. We believe that a minimum of three steps are necessary in respect to their managerial styles as against entrepreneurial role.

i. The succession should not be predetermined and it should not be reserved for members of the family. The CEO must be chosen for his suitability for the position and not because of blood relationship.

ii. The Board should perform a supervisory function with "professional" competence. In a large number of cases friends and relations are appointed on the Board. There is also cross membership among friendly businesses. The CEOs of companies serve on each others Board. In most cases they have limited time to devote to the affairs of the enterprise. The sub-committees exist but are indifferent towards job performance. This situation is not limited to family business alone; it is prevalent in other private businesses also. The role of the Board in crucial but it is rare that the members are chosen who function independently and give enough time and attention of question thoroughly the operational aspects of the organisation.

iii. The third condition is more difficult but we believe important. While occupying an executive position the family members will have to recognise that they hold an executive position and not one of owner-executive. We have observed that many owner-mangers behave like proprietors and not position holders. If he is unable to shed the owner identity they would not be able to establish cooperation and communication that the organisation has to develop. A few individuals have been able to develop this kind of relationship like Vikram Lal in Eicher, family members in TVS and Amalgamated Group and some others. Some of the outstanding leaders like Sir Shri Ram were respected because they had developed family like environment in the business and they were seen as head of this family. At present this tradition does not exist among most entrepreneurs. He developed individuals to hold General Manager positions and as head of the family he inculcated a culture of looking after people and advised individuals without interfering with their day-to-day work and also enouraged discussion.

Chapter 4

Managing Styles of Multinationals

We conducted in-depth interviews with Chief Executives of eight multinationals from different countries and in some cases their employees at different levels of hierarchy. We identified companies which had established their operations in the 1990s and those which had been operating in India for 25 years or more. Wherever it was possible we identified companies in these two categories from the same host country. The purpose of doing this was to compare the styles of managment in long established companies with those which had come in the 90s, post-liberalisation of Indian economy. The eight companies who responded to our request for detailed interviews are from the following countries:-

Group-I : Companies established in 1990s

- Japan
- Korea

- United States
- Germany

Group-II : Companies operating in India for 25 years or more

- United Kingdom (2 companies in different product groups)
- Japan
- Netherlands

Generalisation of Styles

The UK company has operated for many years in the country and their headquarter in UK has given total autonomy to the unit to develop their own systems as per local situation except in terms of certain standard reports. The CEO mentioned that the local company has evolved certain practices and ways of behaviour. The practices have changed and modified according to the conditions prevailing in the country. Generally the home offices of these companies were mainly concerned with financial performance, movement of senior personnel and product diversification. Hence the home office paid attention to the practices and policies relating to the two top levels of management. They obtained reports about their annual assessment by local management and asked for other relevant details as and when required by the home office.

The reporting systems to the home company are followed by companies in this group as well. The performance parameters and the nature of evaluation reports are invariably prescribed by home office and are followed by the companies. The organisations from the United Kingdom had far greater flexibility in respect to country-related matters. The organisations from United States and Netherlands had relatively less flexibility in respect to business and people related matters. The Japanese and the Korean organisations had greater inflexibility in this group of companies.

Some Common Characteristics

i. Irrespective of the operational inflexibility, the home office serves as a frame of reference for these companies; not the local organisations.

ii. The matters relating to senior level personnel are guided, and invariably decided by the home office in consultation with the local management. For example,-decisions on postings in other countries, salary structure and perquisites and management development of senior personnel are guided by the home office.

iii. All investment, diversification and product development matters require home office decisions and concurrence.

iv. Most companies have rigorous programme of induction for employees at entry level to familiarize them with the expectations of the company. Action is promptly taken for deviant behaviour.

v. As the company practices follow orientation of the home company, there is little evidence to integrate the local culture and tradition with management systems and practices in the host country. The predominant concern of the local management and the managers is with performance and results. Most employees reported that they felt the work was stressful and it leaves them with a feeling of anxiousness.

The Companies Established in 1990s

The Primary reason for companies to come to foreign lands is to explore commercial opportunities to strengthen the company's business standing globally. So far most multinationals in developing countries have come from industrially established countries which have strong technology and product superiority. This position is slowly changing and reverse trends are also seen in some of the developing countries notably China, India, Indonesia and others, who are expanding their business interests beyond their shores. The expatriate companies bring their organisational and management practices from their home companies. With increasing global operations and IT support, the home office has standardised all their performance and financial returns so as to compare results of their units located in different countries. The newly established companies also institute their supervisory practices, behaviour patterns, discipline and performance standards based on such practices in their own countries. They invariably provide training to employees based on practices in the home office.

The practices followed by expatriate organisations emanate from their own socio-cultural orientation. In most companies in our sample the practices followed were alien to the Indian ways of life. The conformity to impose practices is in a sense compensated by financial incentives. The salary and incentives earned by employees are much higher than prevailing in most Indian managed companies. Hence employees follow the behaviour patterns required by the company which are in most cases different from their family environment. The dichotomy between the work and the family culture and environment is stressful for most employees. This is what a large number of employees mentioned in our interviews.

Indians like to belong to social groups. At work, frequent interactions with colleagues and people around them is common in most organisations. Even in factories the employees form social groupings (Sheth, 1968). Similar patterns are observed in educational institutions. In the Western sense, privacy for Indians is at best an urban upper middle class phenomenon. In the West, social and work roles are perceived as different roles. In India—the two roles are not differentiated, if someone belongs to a social group the expectation is that at work special considerations will be extended to other members in their work roles as well. As the employment situation in countries such as India improve, and economy develops on a sustained basis, financial incentives alone will not be able to attract the best talent and retain them.

The research team believes that the foreign multinationals in India will have to pay far more attention in adjusting to the wider culture of the society than they appear to do at present. The same consideration will apply to Indian companies when they set up their businesses in other countries. The recent interest in diversity management is an index of this phenomena. A diverse group with varied cultural background can be disruptive for harmonious relationships or they can add value to the decision making process in the organisation. In United States a large number of organisations employ individuals with diverse cultural orientation because work groups with diverse cultural bases have contributed to the quality of their performance. These organisations have taken-up special programmes for managing diversity. The research team believes that as economic performance in India improves, special attention to understanding significant characteristics of the local culture and tradition and their implications for evolving management systems and operating practices would have to be understood by the foreign management. The companies would have to evolve culture-specific systems to improve performance. The existing approach to impose management practices from the Home environment would in some ways become an handicap for attracting and retaining the best people in the organisation.

We found many common practices in Group I companies which came to India in the 1990s.

i. The operating practices followed by the companies were largely adapted from their Home countries. These practices are vigorously followed in factory operations and reporting practices relating to performance and financial matters. As most returns are standardised for purposes of global comparisons by the home offices and communicated through electronic media, the conformity in these practices is considered essential.
ii. The conformity in behaviour and matters of discipline are also drawn from the experience of top and senior managers from the home office. The conformity is achieved through a detailed exercise in the induction programme for employees at entry level, financial incentives for performance and behaviour and decisive action taken in the event of deviant action or behaviour.
iii. The management at all levels believes in employment as a contract between the management and employees. While this is not mentioned in a written down contract but the idea is conveyed in conversation and behaviour viz., the company pays for the quantum and the quality of work that the employee gives to the company. This approach invariably conveys that any personal family

related issues are the responsibility of the employee, and such matters should not in any way influence work for which the company pays a salary.

iv. The total income per employee in multinational companies is considerably higher compared to similarly placed local companies.

v. Most multinational companies provide skill or trade training and require multi-skills in production shops, and in office jobs.

vi. At the operating level, especially in the manufacturing units supervision is close. The inspection schedules are also detailed.

vii. The selection procedures for recruitment at all levels are formalised and followed.

The common features identified are practiced by these companies. The approaches mentioned here varied in degree from one company to another. But in essential terms the approaches outlined above are applicable to most companies.

The Management Styles

As mentioned earlier companies followed their home office styles of management and the past experience of the expatriates as a model. In some cases even when the chief executive was of Indian origin, he was following the home office styles of management either because of his long years of working in the home office or that he believed that home office systemis should be followed for achieving results. Even the Indian managers in multinationals imbibe the style from their supervisors. When they were asked why their approaches are different from managers in Indian owned companies, two types of responses came from them. Some said that by following the company mode they are able to get results, and a few others said that they will not progress in their careers if they did not conform to what they believed was expected of them by the company. In this sense there is a conscious, and perhaps in some cases unconscious effort to create a culture of conformity and performance. These are valued. Most executives work long hours and seem to operate under pressure. Some managers were more open and stated that they do not like work as they are always under pressure of competing with others. When we asked them what induces them to continue in their jobs, the reply invariably was that there is good money and perks and they cannot find another place with comparable financial advantages.

In most companies, business and social interaction is largely with client organisations or other multinationals. Some executives create their own niche in professional bodies. The expatriate staff invariably create their own social circle among themselves, as do the native employees.

The CEO of companies from China, Japan, UK, USA were interviewed in depth. The companies managed by Japan, USA and China had been established in the last ten years or so. Except the UK based company the other three tend to install the practices in terms of work procedures, organisation of task, supervision, control, discipline, behaviour at work, etc. Employees conform to the demands of the organisation because as mentioned earlier their take-home packet in most cases is bigger than the average available for industry. There is also fear of severe action for deviating from the laid down rules and procedures. The important consideration is that the work culture and need for conformity to organisational requirements are different from those prevailing in the society. Employees conform to one set of bevahioural norms at home and society and another set at work. It is open to study whether the situation leads to mental health problems. For a conclusive view on this matter we were not able to callect sufficient data from our interviews (JBP Sinha, 2000).

The cross-culture literature suggests that Japanese Korean and other Asian Countries like China, Indonesia etc., have close relationships with employees (JBP Sinha, 2000). In our discussions with chief executives and other managers, we found that there was no serious concern for understanding the Indian social-cultural milieu, except in a general way. Rather the emphasis was on the commercial matters and how best hurdles can be overcome whenever they come in the way of business.

The Implications

The multinationals operating in India seem to be primarily concerned with commercial operations. The companies which have manufacturing operations have responsibility for adaptation of the items that they manufacture for Indian conditions but research is primarily the concern of the home office.

There is little evidence in our sample of companies to recognise the socio-cultural milieu of the Indian society. Rather these companies secure conformity by employing two potent measures: one, financial incentives, and two, strict discipline. We surmise that as economic conditions in the country improve the financial incentives will have somewhat limited response. Another factor that contributes to conformity by employees has to do with better relative impersonality in relationships among supervisors and their employees. The gap is wider between senior and middle levels of managers in relationships. It is more formal compared to Indian owned and managed organisations. However, relationships are more relaxed in multinationals that have been established for longer years in India. In all these aspects the management focus on performance is sharp. The home offices expect high returns and measure effectiveness in financial returns.

The experience of Indian companies to acquire substantial interests abroad is relatively new. The branches of the banks in USA and Europe and construction projects in middle-east have largely employed ethnic population. The research team has elaborated some issues and problems in operating abroad in Chapter-7.

Chapter 5

The Management Styles of Public Sector Enterprises

Public Sector is seen to be an instrument of the economic policy of the Government. As such it is regulated and directed by the Government and the Ministry under which it falls provides overall direction. These enterprises are subject to overall policies of the Government in respect to public enterprises, and the concerned Ministry. However, most public enterprises are registered as Public Limited Companies and provisions of the Company Act apply to their operations. They have Board of Governors with a Chairman as do privately owned and managed companies. While this multi-governance exists, operationally the real regulatory authority lies with the concerned Ministry within overall policy framework of the Government. In this sense the management of the public sector enterprises has characteristics at the top levels of management similar to that of the family managed enterprises. In the latter case the family exercises final and in most cases over-riding control as does the concerned ministry of the Government in the case of public enterprises. The critical difference between the two is that Government consists of many departments and people who frequently change. The family has continuity.

The Management Style

It is unrealistic to consider all public enterprises in the same basket. There are some enterprises which have history of sustained outstanding performance and there are some others that have periods of excellence and then a drop in their performance or the other way round. There are a very large number of enterprises which have either average or below average performance. Notwithstanding the differences, public enterprises have many common characteristics.

i. With a rare exception, public enterprises have followed the Government pattern of vertical functional control. Each function has independent structure. As in Government, coordination between bureaus is achieved at higher levels of managerial hierarchy.

ii. The authority flows downward from top levels of the hierarchy. In this sense the critical and many operating decisions rest with higher levels of management, even when the powers are formally delegated to every position. The managers and supervisory personnel have a built-in tendency to "play-safe" in decision making, each seeking patronage of his supervisors. There is general tendency to seek "god-fathers" in the organisation for survival. In this respect, essentially the organisational functioning is similar to that of family managed organisations.

iii. Relationships are primarily governed by rules and regulations that are articulated in the conduct rules and by notification from higher authority.

iv. The trade unions have a decisive influence on the system. This influence is critical largely an account of the size of the enterprises and more importantly because in most cases the union leadership has direct access to the political leaders who lead the Government. There is commonality among the union leadership and the political party who have to rely on the votes of the people that the unions command. In most cases informal channels are used to influence decision making at enterprise level. These aspects cannot be ignored by the enterprise management. This situation varies from time to time depending on the nature and strength of the political leadership in the Government.

v. In most enterprises the personnel management is modelled after the Government system. The conflict management is weak. There is marked tendency to avoid conflict and play safe. Supervisors are known to advise their managers to "be tactful". Hence, managers often allow adverse situations to drift rather than confront and seek realistic resolution of relationship problems. In our interviews we found that most managers seek posting in advisory or specialist functions to get away from the pressures of unions and that of many other external agencies.

vi. The managers also feel the need for a collective representative body to seek protection from arbitrary action. Hence almost all public enterprises have unit level union-like Associations of supervisory personnel. These Associations also have a national level collective organisation.

vii. Age and seniority are valued in promotions and career decisions. In some enterprises the merit is indirectly rewarded by giving special consideration to batches by year of employment and within this the best among them are given preference.

Our interview data shows that a large number of managers seek employment in public enterprises because of a combination of considerations. The most important among these are: feeling of national service, security of employment, protection from arbitrary action by higher level officials.

While the common characteristics of the public-enterprises may give the impression that the executives would be unable to respond to market changes, and would be lost in routine of the task in hand, there are many that have shown increasing and sustained dynamism. Some have innovated and competed with the best in the industry, and excelled in international competition. Some companies have grown rapidly in high technology processes. They have been market leaders either over a sustained period of time or at some stages of their history. Hence the research team tried to understand the reasons that contributed towards the organisation becoming a market leader. We studied specifically five such organisations and identified what seemed like the common characteristics among them.

i. The chief executives wanted to build organisational capabilities and not be satisfied merely by maintaining the system. The capability building included people development, the operating processes, the technology and related functions.

ii. They were concerned with problem-resolution rather than drift. They were willing to face problems involved in working through the problem areas.

iii. They were respected by managers within the organisation and took pains to deal with external influences including the pressures from the Government and the public.

iv. They encouraged senior managers to associate freely with professional bodies and seek help from outside experts where required.

v. They were open to experimentation, e.g. try out new ways of handling problems to the extent new ideas needed trying out.

vi. They took stock of problems that inhibited performance and dealt with a whole range of problems simultaneously e. g. followed systems and not segmental approach to problem diagnosis and action.

vii. While the chief executive took the initiative, the senior levels of managers were consulted. They encouraged discussion among managers. There was a distinct attempt to obtain consensus among various groups in the ogranisation. In addition an action group was created to follow up the plans and this group met the chief executive regularly.

The organisation invariably obtained help from external bodies. In some cases internal teams were appointed to serve as internal expert body.

Strengths and Weaknesses

Strengths and Weaknesses of the public sector organisations have to be seen in the context of the State Policy which initiated the setting up of such enterprises. Public policy aims at economic, social and public welfare aspects. The public related policies invariably take both a short and a long term perspective. As visualised in various policy resolutions of the Government on the subject, the public enterprises were set up to build an industrial base in the country, dispersed growth centers for industrial development and creating employment opportunities for citizens at all levels. Broadly, until 1980s the many statements by concerned Ministries included all these aspects. The poor economic performance of the country in the 1980s and beyond, the Government placed greater emphasis on profitability and ROI. Certain privileges and relative autonomy for decision making were extended to profit making public enterprises. The subsidy in most cases was withdrawn. Hence the evaluation of public enterprises in the 90s and beyond rated various aspects of return on investment. As compared with private businesses the public enterprises on the whole showed poorer returns. This concern became sharper because barring a few profit making companies, a large number needed financial support from Government. With liberalising trade and business many of the not so well performing companies were hit further in their markets. Most of them had failed to upgrade technology, work systems or managerial practices. Bearing this background in mind, the strengths and weaknesses of the public sector enterprises in broad terms are identified below:-

Strengths

Public sector enterprises have laid strong foundation for manufacturing competence in the country which has given the country an edge in this area of business.They have made available to the country:-

i. a vast manpower with expertise in most areas of engineering, electronics, heavy and light industry, including financial services, In fact most industries in private businesses have attracted the manpower from pubic enterprises,

ii. new and improved technologies and in many cases some enterprises improved upon them,

iii. built strong institutions for training of workers, technicians and managers in technical occupations and management,

iv. developed R&D facilities in engineering, chemical technology and refinery,

v. thrown up some outstanding individuals in technical and general management who have in many cases moved on to set up new businesses, thus increasing the industrial base in the country.

vi. some of the better managed and better performing public enterprises have developed capacity and competence to compete in global markets and assure leadership role in command areas,

vii. built colonies for housing their employees and medical facilities which are open to outsiders as well.

The contribution listed here varies vastly from one enterprise to another. On the whole the public sector enterprises in manufacturing sector and family owned businesses in certain sectors, specially trading and commerce have given India a strong foundation for development in the last 15 years or so.

Weaknesses

i. Barring a certain number of companies who have done well in economic, public service and entrepreneurial role, a large number have relied heavily on Government patronage and financial support instead of building up their own capacity and market potential.

ii. Inadequate attention has been given to evolve a composite criteria for measuring effectiveness of public enterprises. For example, in early years social responsibility was emphasised while in later years economic performance has been used to rate these enterprises.

iv. The lack of discipline by Ministries to clarify and follow the demarcation of responsibility by the Board and the Ministry made the role of Boards somewhat redundant, denying effective supervisory and directional support to the enterprise.

v. The failure to develop organisational and management practices suited to the task in which they are engaged instead of the bureaucratic structure and functions that characterise them. Lack of this has impeded their ability to adjust to market situations. In economy of shortages, they were able to dominate the market in their product group but in competitive environment they are far too inflexible to change with market demands. Some of them have succeeded because of their technical base or the outstanding leadership of some people at the top.

vi. Over time the pure intentions of setting up public enterprises became diffused and many decisions to set up new enterprises were governed by vested interests of political and administrative heads. They became a source of bestowing favours to some individuals. The appointments were made without analysing the particular needs of the concerned enterprise. The government is credited with many reforms to remove the infirmities but people have ways of defeating regulations by ingenious ways. As Roethlisberger said many years ago, human problems cannot be resolved by other than human ways. The experience of Enron confirms that when people at higher levels intend to do something right or wrong they can find ways to do them.

vi. Among the many reforms the Government has initiated the currently practiced system of developing an MoU between the enterprise and the administrative ministry has potential for success. It commits both the PSU and the concerned Ministry to the agreed performance standard and the nature of support that would be provided by the Ministry. An expert body mediates between the two to finalise the MoU. The results are also reviewed by the expert body. This system was started in the latter half of the 1980s. Inspite of the system being elaborate, it has over the years become largely a budgetary exercise and in many cases commitments are not honoured or taken seriously. These criticisms are voiced in many review reports on the subject.

As mentioned in speeches of Prime Minister Jawaharlal Nehru and many other Ministers the intention of the Government was to register PSUs under Company Legislation so that they should function independently as commercial entities. The logic was that Government systems were too restrictive to operate in market environment. In the early 1970s the Industry Minister, Kumaramangalam initiated the holding company pattern under which the Chairman of the Company would also function as Secretary of Government of India. In operational terms however the PSEs failed to evolve their own independent managerial systems and practices to respond to market situations. Instead they evolved bureaucratic systems of managing, patterned after the government. Added to this, Indians in positions of authority have strong need to control people. Psychological studies have shown that Indians have high power needs. Tandon has described his experience as Chairman of State Trading Corporation (STC). In one instance he has mentioned that even under or deputy secretaries in the Ministry expected senior managers in PSEs to respect their directives and requests over telephones. Failure to do so invited adverse reactions (Tondon, 1971). This feeling was expressed by many managers in PSEs. Perhaps without the expressed intention to do so, the PSEs in many operational terms became 'attached offices' of the Ministry.

Inspite of these limitations some public enterprises have achieved impressive results and contributed significantly towards industrial strength acquired by the country. Some of these achievements are listed earlier in the section on strengths of public enterprises.

What can be done in Respect to Future Development

The founding fathers had comprehensive perspective of society in which disparities among different segments of the population is minimal and the nation as a whole should develop. A citizen should have a livelihood, education, health care, housing and the freedom to be himself in terms of religion, beliefs and opportunity for advancement. These considerations are reflected in the constitution of the country and a vast number of varied institutions are created for achievement of these objectives.

The public sector has to be seen in the overall context of national development. The supervisory role of the Government should be seen within this frame. The problems of autonomy for enterprises and control by Government, has to maintain a balance in respect to two questions.

i. What are the management systems and policies needed for an enterprise to achieve the goals set out in the development context.
ii. How should national goals be integrated with the individual goals of the enterprise and to what extent and in what manner the assumptions underlying the policy and functions of the enterprise need to be regulated by the Government.

The questions so conceived provide a distinct role to both the enterprise and the government. However the government ministries in most cases began to perform a supervisory role that should be performed by the Governing Board. Because the CEO's future and basic support depended on the Administrative Ministry, the people in the enterprises established a kind of reciprocity with Ministries where each did favours to the other. In this process the Governing Boards were left with somewhat limited function. One has to look at the minutes of the Board meetings where most important decisions came up mainly for ratification, and not discussion and decision. This situation did not prevail in enterprises which had leadership recognised for their outstanding performance and had direct access to the political decision makers. Hence the first condition for public enterprises to effectively perform the role for which they are set up, is to clarify the role and the limits of the Governing Board. Not the Ministry but the Governing Board should be responsible for performance of the enterprise while the government should supervise its linkage with national policies and plans. The Government should certainly raise questions with the Board, not the CEO alone in respect to their plans of development, technology upgradation, R&D systems and any other aspects that seem crucial for operational efficiency and sustained growth. The appointments to the Boards are at present, at least in a large number of cases, made on the basis of "personal choice" or convenience. The constitution of the Board should be based on two considerations. One, what are the nature of problems that need expertise and advise, and two, who are the people known for expertise in the areas that need strengthening in the particular PSE.

The experience of change in large organisations in India and abroad suggest that piecemeal changes rarely give desired results. Rather simultaneous changes in at least key areas of the enterprise are necessary, including changes in the minds of people engaged in the effort. At the minimum simultaneous action in the following areas is necessary to bring about a culture of achievement.

i. Clear understanding of the role of the Ministry, the Governing Board and that of the enterprise management is necessary. The Board functions and the manning of the Boards need clarity and above all acceptance by the parties concerned.

ii. Shift from bureaucratic to a more commercially oriented system has to be evolved for competing in emerging market situation.

iii. There is little effort in appointing top level managerial personnel to identify specific problem areas of a PSE and to match the quality of leadership required to cope successfully with the problems. In the bureaucratic system prevailing in public sector enterprises the leader-quality and his acceptance, and reach, to political leadership is important. There is little evidence that sufficient time and study is given to the installation of management.

iv. A significant departure from the existing practice was planned by Former Prime Minister, Rajiv Gandhi's Government in late 1980s but it was never put into practice. The Public Sector Selection Board was required to identify people related problem areas and measures to develop human potential is PSUs.

v. Special consideration is necessary for strengthening R&D, technology and market-related functions. Some of the best performing public enterprises have done so, to substantiate the point a few names can be mentioned Bharat Electronics (BEL), Bharat Heavy Engineering Industries (BHEL), Steel Authority of India (SAIL), GAIL and National Thermal Power Corporation (NTPC) and the PSUs in the petroleum and the oil sectors.

It is perhaps recognised but deserve repeating that no arrangement can work unless people in leadership positions consciously exercise self-restraint, and encourage people to develop their own potential.

vi. The Chief Executives and the senior personnel should be required to take at least one week away in a training programme on Leader Effectiveness. Top down leader style may achieve results in the short term but it does not contribute to building a stable and dynamic system.

The suggestions made here are not new. They are contained in a large number of commissions and committees for reforms in the public sector enterprises. Partly due to vested interests in perpetuating the arrangement on the part of the political and the administrative systems and partly due to the enormity of the task, suggestions are examined by expert bodies and often relegated to history.

Chapter 6

Job Satisfaction and Organisational Culture

Organisations exist to persist. Besides the market forces, the perpetuation of organisation depends on its internal environment. In addition to profit optimisation, quality assurance and competition, organisation would have to devote their time and energy in reinforcing organizational culture and provide sufficient room to employees to derive satisfaction from their jobs. This chapter examines the level of job satisfaction of employees in three organisations (family owned organisation, BPOs, and a large telecom company) operating in India and its effect on organisational culture.

Job Satisfaction

The term job satisfaction was brought to limelight by Hoppock (1935). He reviewed 32 studies on job satisfaction conducted prior to 1933 and observed that job satisfaction is a combination of psychological, physiological and environmental circumstances that cause a person to say—"I am satisfied with my job". Such a description indicates the variety of variables that influence the satisfaction of the individual but tell us nothing about the nature of job satisfaction. Perhaps, one way to define job satisfaction may be to say that it is the end state of feeling about the job and the organisation. Notice the use of the word end. It emphasises the fact that the feeling is experienced after a task is accomplished or an activity has taken place whether it is highly individualistic effort of writing a book or a collective endeavour of constructing a dam. These tasks/ activities could be very minute or large. They may be easily observable or could just be experienced. But in all cases, they satisfy a certain need. The feeling could be positive or negative depending upon whether the need is satisfied or not and could be a function of the efforts of the individual on the one hand, and on the other the situational opportunities available to him.

Job satisfaction has been regarded both as a general attitude as well as satisfaction with specific dimensions of the job such as pay, the work itself, promotion opportunities, supervision, co-workers and so forth. These may interact in different ways to create the feeling of satisfaction with the job. The degree of satisfaction may vary with how well the outcomes fulfill or exceed expectations. Mumford (1991) analysed job satisfaction in two ways. First, in terms of the fit between what the organisation requires and what the employee is seeking and second, in terms of the fit between what the employee is seeking and what he/she is actually receiving. Work is inextricably bound with human existence. The content and context of work should therefore promote, rather than damage human dignity. Kanungo (1992) pointed out that managers have the moral obligation to empower subordinates and thereby promote their growth and development. He strongly emphasises the need to analyse work norms and conditions, to see whether such practices promote productive behaviour, high job satisfaction, and overall improvement of work life and that they are consistent with the dignity of the employees as human beings.

Organisational Culture

Culture is a very powerful force at work place, which is consciously cultivated and passed on to employees from one generation to the next. Organizational culture refers to the psychological environment in which the behaviour of the organisational member occurs. The essential core of culture consists of traditional (i.e. historically derived and selected) ideas and specially the value attached to them. Culture system may be considered both as product of action and as conditioning elements of future actions. In the words of Hofstede (1980) culture is a collective programming of the mind, which "distinguishes the members of one human group from another". The Indian perspective suggests that "Culture consists of totality of assumptions, beliefs, values, social systems and institutions, physical artifacts and behaviour of people reflecting their desire to maintain continuity as well as to adopt to external demands" (Sinha 2000). It is the shared understanding, which is an essential component of organisational cultures.

Based on the general frame as suggested by Hofstede and Sinha, organizational culture was indexed in terms of the following five dimensions.

Adaptability:

Ability to accommodate differences and adapt themselves to the demands that arise in family, life and work situations as against controlling others.

Collectivism:

Sense of family, community, work group commitment even at the cost of personal hardship and sacrifice.

Obedience to Elders:

Acceptance of prescribed roles without questioning them. Age and seniority more important than merit of individual.

Dependence Proneness:

Tendency to accept and not voice opinions contrary to those expressed by people in higher positions and roles.

Belief in Fate:

Faith in destiny and predetermined life cycle, hence lack of will to compete or make effort to work for success.

Methodology

Measure of Dimensions:

Based on the descriptions of the five dimensions a number of statements purported to measure these dimensions were developed. These statements were discussed by members of the research team and those that were found to have face validity pertaining to each of the dimensions were identified. This exercise resulted in two statements per dimension.

Measure of Job Satisfaction:

Survey of the literature on the measurement of job satisfaction reflects the complexity of the process. Some of the methods measure over all job satisfaction, while others look at the satisfaction with specific aspects of the job. Since satisfaction with one aspect of the job may be difficult to isolate because of the complex ways it is intercorrelated with other facets of the job, an overall measure of job satisfaction may provide more reliable data. This is further supported in a study by Wanous and Lawler (1972) who found that 23 operational definitions based on 23 facets of job satisfaction did not yield empirically comparable measures of satisfaction. Some correlated better with the overall rating of job satisfaction than others. Perhaps a more reliable way to measure job satisfaction could be to use more direct approach tapping overall satisfaction. Hence the following four statements were used to measure job satisfaction.

i. I love to come to my factory every day.
ii. I would recommend this job to all my friends and relatives.
iii. If I start my life again, I would definitely choose my persent job.
iv. I am satisfied with my job.

Hindi Version:

Since a large number of respondents did not know English an attempt was made to translate the English version into simple Hindi. A group of individuals efficient in both languages were requested to translate the English version into Hindi. In the second stage another group of individuals well versed in both languages were requested to translate the Hindi version in English. Subsequently the two Hindi versions were compared. In case of discrepancies changes in language were made before a final translation was accepted.

Scale of Measurement The 10 statements measuring five dimensions and four statements measuring job satisfaction were presented to the respondents. They were asked to read each statement carefully and show their degree of agreement/ disagreement with them by using the following six–point scale. In addition to the above, respondents were asked to indicate their age, gender, years of education and years of experience

6 = strongly agree
5 = agree
4 = agree a little
3 = disagree a little
2 = disagree
1 = strongly disagree

In order to get a single measure for each of the 5 dimensions, the two statements for each dimension were intercorrelated for the total sample. The values of coefficient along with dimensions are presented below:

Adaptability	$r = .213; p < .01$
Collectivism	$r = .318; p < .01$
Obedience to elders	$r = .303; p < .01$
Dependence Proneness	$r = .252; p < .01$
Belief in Fate	$r = .238; p < .01$

The values of all coefficients are significant suggesting thereby that the scores on two items can be added to get a single measure for each of the **5** dimensions.

Job Satisfaction

As far as the job satisfaction statements are concerned, all four of them were Intercorrelated to get a single score for job satisfaction. The values of coefficient are given below.

Statement 1 vs 2	r = .167;p < .01
Statement 1 vs 3	r = .159;p < .01
Statement 1 vs 4	r = .206;p < .01
Statement 1 vs 3	r = .580;p < .01
Statement 1 vs 4	r = .341;p < .01
Statement 1 vs 4	r = .545;p < .01

Since all the statements measuring job satisfaction correlated significantly with each other, individual scores were combined together to get a single measure of job satisfaction. The total value ranged between 4-24.

Sample

Since the objective of the study was to compare job satisfaction across organisations and its relation with organisation culture indices, data was collected from three organisations. Their brief profiles are presented below:-

Family Owned Organisation:

Two family owned organisations (FOO) Atlas Cycle and Kamla Dials and Devices Ltd. participated in this study. Atlas Cycle (AC) started way back in 1951. Being a family managed organisation, decisions of the elders are respected. It has four units and produces 2,00,0000 cycles per month. Kamla Dials and Devices Ltd. (KDDL) was established in 1983. It manufactures watch dials and watch hands. During 2002-2003 its turnover was 420 million. Both organisations believe in quest for excellence, teamwork and oneness. The corporate philosophy is based on quality, efficiency, self-development, teamwork and fairness. In both cases, organisational culture has a lot to do with family culture. Total loyalty and sincerity is demanded. Ethics, discipline and accessibility are the key values. Both believe in transparency and differences are dealt in open. Both give the feelings to employees that; "we are family and cannot do without each other".

Business Process Outsourcing :

Business Process Outsourcing (BPO) is comparatively a recent introduction to the world of career options in India. The career avenues are provided by call centers, a trend started by GE when it established a call centre near New Delhi in 1998. These 'new workplaces' are characterised by 'flat' and non-bureaucratic organisational structures, informal relationships, emphasis on teamwork, and flexible management policies. Most IT companies, both Indian and MNC, offer relatively non-hierarchical work cultures, employee-friendly human resource policies, attractive working environment and high salaries. But at the same time, the industry is known for its high-pressure work atmosphere and long working hours, which create high levels of stress, employee dissatisfaction, and high attrition rates. BPOs employ a mix of 'direct' and 'indirect' or 'normative' methods of organisational control. Indirect forms of control derive from contemporary management theories in the West, and are more humane and employee-friendly than the direct methods of bureaucratic control and include the creation of a strong corporate culture and organisation into teams. In the BPO industries, the relationship between management and employees is less formal because the educational, social class and age differences between employees and managers are minimal. These factors mitigate against possible conflict between employees and managements, and explain the general lack of interest in unionisation or collective action in this industry. Employees tend to deal with management as a individual, and when they are not satisfied with their jobs they vote with their feet, contributing to the high attrition rate for which the industry is known.

Telecom Organisation (TO)

Established in the year 1987, TO has developed a vast base for indigenous telecom equipment manufacturing in India. It started with manufacturing transmission equipment and soon expanded its product portfolio to Manufacture Access Equipment, Optical Fiber Cable, Accessories and Terminal Equipment. A combination of long-term vision and proactive business strategy has helped TO to achieve a leadership position. From the time of inception, intensive R&D efforts have helped to create products that match global standards. Today it has grown from a single-product, single-customer to a multi-product, multi-customer company. The R&D areas range from exploration of new technologies, designing of radio, optical transmission equipment and access equipment and development of software solutions that include a high level of network management system. TO reputation is built upon its technological expertise and in its sophisticated manufacturing plants. It believes in optimum capacity utilisation and minimum wastage. With strength of more than 1500 professionals, TO has made footprints countrywide having over 20 offices to reach every type of telecom customer for pre sales liaison, technical support, post sales warranty and AMC support. It provides complete customer satisfaction by providing constant support in the shortest possible time.

Data Collection

Data was collected by seeking the cooperation of the employees. They filled out the questionnaire either in their office/workstation or in small groups. They had the choice to fill out either the Hindi or the English version. The final sample consisted of 394 respondents from FOO, 45 from BPO and 65 from TO.

Results

This section presents the sample profile of the respondents and the results of the study. Table-1 presents the sample profile.

Table-1

Sample Profile

Variables	FOO			BPO			TO		
	N	M	SD	N	M	SD	N	M	SD
Age	394	33.40	7.245	43	25.32	3.103	44	24.79	2.179
Education	394	13.31	3.200	41	16.44	1.322	51	15.74	7.725
Experience	392	10.61	6.572	37	4.46	3.691	58	2.96	2.290
Gender									
M		96.2%			25.6%			50.0%	
F		03.8%			74.4%			50.0%	

N= Number of Respondents; M=average; SD= Standard Deviation Estimate.

Results on age show that the employees of FOO are much older as compared to those in BPO or TO. However high standard deviation for FOO shows that the variations in age could be high. Unlike the general conception, BPO employees have 16.4 years of formal education which is followed by those in TO and FOO. The employees of TO have an average of about 3 years of work experience while .those with FOO have a little more than 10 years of experience. Most employees in FOO are male while the female employees are in majority in BPO. For TO the distribution is half and half. The average and standard deviation estimates of job satisfaction for 3 organisations are given in Table-2.

Table-2

Job Satisfaction

Value	FOO	BPO	TO
N	394	45	65
M	16.59	16.35	9.23
SD	3.575	4.765	2.861

In order to see if the difference in job satisfaction across organizations are significant a one way analysis of variance with unequal sample was size carried out. The results are presented in Table-3.

Table-3

Analysis of Variance

Source	SS	DF	MS	F
Between	2424	2	1212	62.47**
Within	9717	501	19.4	
Total	12141	503		

** P<.01

The results of analysis of variance show significant differences (F=62.47, df 2/501; P<.01) suggesting thereby that the degree of job satisfaction varies amongst the organisations. An examination of averages in Table-2 shows that employees of TO are less satisfied as compared to those in FOO or BPO.

While the five indices of organisational culture intercorelate with each other (see Table-4), they were individually correlated with job satisfaction. The purpose was to see if any one of the indices refers to variation in job satisfaction and if this variation can be attributed to the specifics in organisational culture.

Table-4
Inter-Index Correlation

Index	B	C	D	E
A. Adaptability	0.820	.218**	.260**	.183*
B. Collectivism		.284**	.256*	.286*
C. Obedience			.291**	.237**
D. Dependence				.071
E. Belief in fate				

* P<.05; ** P<.01

Table 5
Job satisfaction & Organizational Culture

Index	FOO	BPO	TO
A. Adoptability	**.289****	**–.403****	**.500****
B. Collectivism	**.286****	**.269**	**.160**
C. Obedience	**.322****	**.060**	**–.422****
D. Dependence	**.211****	**–.295***	**–.151**
E. Belief in fate	**.210***	**–.204**	**.370**

* P<.05; ** P<.01

The result in table 4 and 5 present an unusual picture. While all the indices of organisational culture intercorelate with each other significantly suggestive thereby that all or any one of them can be a measurement of organisational culture, individually they do not seem to correlate with job satisfaction.

As far as family managed organisations are concerned all five indices correlate significantly with job satisfaction. Suggesting thereby the following:

1. The higher the ability to accommodate differences and adapt to the demands in work situations the greater the job satisfaction.
2. Job satisfaction increases with increasing degree of concern for family and community even at the cost of personal hardship and sacrifice.
3. The greater the acceptance of prescribed roles the greater the job satisfaction.
4. The greater the tendency to accept opinion of people in higher positions and not voice once own opinion, the greater the job satisfaction.
5. Those who have faith in destiny and predetermined life cycle are more satisfied with their jobs.

However, when it comes to BPO only two values are significant. Adaptability and Dependence, Both values are in negative direction suggesting thereby that job satisfaction decreases with increasing adaptability and dependence. On the other hand for employees in TO adaptability and belief in fate correlate significantly and in positive direction as in FOO. Obedience negatively but significantly correlates with job satisfaction. All other correlations in both BPO and TO are insignificant.

Disussion

This study was conducted to examine variations in the level of job satisfaction across three kinds of organisations and the relationship of the job satisfaction with 5 indices of organsational culture. Family owned organisations seem to inculcate some degree of job satisfaction amongst their employees. Perhaps it is the general considerate style of management in these organisations that leads to significant levels of job satisfaction on all indices. Two significant values of coefficient for BPO are in the negative direction. Employees do not seem to be very happy if they have to accommodate differences and are unable to voice their opinion. However when contrasted with TO, the level of job satisfaction at TO seems to be quite low. Perhaps the focus on professionalism and maintaining and/ or inventing new kind of technology (Products) at fast pace puts tremendous pressure on employees which results in lack of adequate satisfaction with the job. Telecommunication is becoming a highly competitive business with so many organisations providing the same service. Hence the pressure to keep up with competition or even to surpass it could make an individual burnout fast. Flexibility, freedom and control on one's pace of activity are important inputs in ensuring job satisfaction. Their absence may shift the focus to seek satisfaction elsewhere i.e. other than the job.

Family owned organisations generally reflect the prevalent societal expectations, norms and values. A person born and brought up in a particular society feels very comfortable with organisations that practice the same culture that is available in life in general. The transfer from society to organisation is easy as the induction process only reinforces the value system that the person has already acquired. A case of Japanese society getting in Japanese organisation is common knowledge. Adaptability, collectivism, obedience, dependence and belief in fate are prevalent social norms in India. Management practices that are consistent with these norms help employees to adapt to organisational expectations, leading to high degree of job satisfaction. This seems to be true as far as FOO is concerned. However adaptability and dependence seem to militate against the organisational expectation as far as BPOs are concerned, leading to inverse relationship between them and job satisfaction. Employee controlling one's own situation and voicing ones own opinion, is the price that BPO industry has to pay, TO over the years has not been able to perform well. Those who have followed the prescribed rules have done so to survive in the organisation but it has resulted in dissatisfaction with the job. Hence we have a significant but negative relationship between job satisfaction and obedience ($r = .422$, off = 63, $p < .01$).

Chapter 7

Preparing for New Challenges

Earlier chapters have referred to the imperatives of the emerging economic and business environment for organisations. The demands of business would be more exacting than what was faced by management in the regulated market environment. Almost all functions would have to respond to the market realities of the situation. Response of individuals and employees at all levels would finally determine the competitive position of an organisation. All aspects of business operations, managerial systems and leadership would have to reorient to meet market demands and develop required practices and processes. All development efforts depend on the cooperation of people at all levels and among themselves. This single factor to a large extent would contribute to the strength and capability of the organisation to cope with the market situation. This chapter is concerned with what is involved in building this capability within the organisation. However important technology and knowledge management may be, their advantage to the organisation would depend on the readiness of people to absorb these and employ them optimally.

What is Expected from Employees

The survival strength of organisations depends on their ability to optimise efficiency of operations, continuous improvement in all aspects of work, ability to innovate and adapt to the changing demands of markets. These aspects require willingness of people at all levels to anticipate requirements and change the internal arrangements to effectively respond to the external requirements. The President of Bell Telephones in the United States, Chester Barnard in mid 1930s had said that "willingness of people to contribute effort to the cooperative system is necessary to achieve organisational goals" (Barnard, 1938). Katz and Kahn in their monumental work on organisational role had drawn a distinction between 'dependable role performance' and 'innovative and spontaneous behaviour'. (Katz and Kahn, 1966). This distinction is most important in examining the organisational response to the market situation. The implication here is that individuals and groups should want to cooperate and this element of wanting has to come from within, hence the question is what should an organization do to make this happen.

The noted psychologist Herzberg had formulated what is referred to as two factor theory of motivation. The theory has emerged from the analysis of responses of people at work. Herzberg suggests that workers need certain minimum conditions at work such as supportive supervision, interpersonal relations, salary and adequacy of working conditions. These are desirable for

people to work. However, these conditions do not by themselves lead to an individual's involvement in work. Rather the factors that motivate people are those that require an individual's own capabilities and visible outcome of his effort. These are in essence a sense of achievement, recognition and work itself. In substance the involvement of individuals is possible by creating such conditions by designing work that provide motivational factors. A person or a group should be able to exercise discretion in executing the assigned task. Where possible, an individual or a group should be able to see results of what he or she does. The reward, the recognition, and advancement should be associated with the achievement of results (Herzberg 1966: Rice, 1958 : Reddin 1987; Dayal, 2006). This consideration is applicable to individuals irrespective of educational level, hierarchy, age or any other such factors. Based on this concept Reddin, a well recognised consultant, developed a scheme to organise and define jobs at all levels such that the outcome of every job is clearly established and therefore, measured (Reddin, 1987). Lord Wilfred Brown, as Chairmen of Glacier Metal Works in London and a noted psycholoanalyst Elliott Jacques reorganised and defined jobs with prescribed and discretionary content (Brown and Jaques, 1965). They stated that if a job has no discretion, it is better to mechanise it. Many of these ideas emerged from the pioneering work on socio-technical systems carried out by scholars at Tavistock Institute of Human Relations in London and job redesign in the US. The work is extensively published and described by Eric Trist, AK Rice, Bamforth, Miller and applications by companies such as GE, ICI, and other. They also undertook consulting projects in India in the 1950s and wrote extensively about the experience in books and articles.
(Rice, 1958; Miller & Rice 1965, and Dayal, 2006).

The emotional and personal involvement in performing a given task is essential for people to be involved in their job. Billy Graham said that hot heads and cold hearts never solved anything. The important consideration is that most organisations will have to collapse levels of hierarchy, be conscious of market demands and give individual responsibility for results. Without such organisational measures, it is unlikely that cost reduction, efficiency and the requisite quality of product and service can be achieved. The research data and experience of companies like GE, Xerox, IBM and others show that individuals take up responsibility for results when they have to exercise discretion in the job assigned to them. In behavioural terms individuals accept responsibility when an individual rather than the machine or the work design has direction of the work that an employee does. A great deal of work in this respect has also been done in several organisations in India (De, 1984; Rice, 1958). Many social scientists have suggested that discretionary element should be built into the job (Jacques, 1965).

LG Electronics in India who are in an extremely competitive consumer durables and entertainment market, undertook what they have called empowerment exercise. Every individual has total responsibility for results in his assigned task. He is given commensurate authority to achieve results. Discretion is built into the job. The company has been able to maintain their leadership position by reducing costs, improving quality and services, to innovate and gain superiority in their markets. (Verma, 2006).

Some Special Considerations in India

The studies of child rearing practices suggest some common behavioural characteristics (Dayal, 1976; Sinha, 1990). The traditional family values and practices that contribute to the individual's emotional self are the following:

i. Collective rather than individual orientation leading to strong bonds with family and the community
ii. Tolerance and accommodation to different people
iii. Respect for age and acceptance of authority
iv. Spirituality-faith in something beyond self

The American literature on management has influenced teaching in almost all management schools throughout the world. The concepts in this literature are developed on the basis of research, informed observations of management practices in the American scene and writings of practicing managers. The orientation and practices in their writings is influenced by the cultural orientation that dominates the people concerned. In broad terms the American orientation is guided by what is referred to in literature as protestant ethics and high social value for individual achievement. The American business over the years has strong values in terms of individualism and as a corollary of this, on competition and winning. The practices in business organisations have also underpinnings of these guiding notions. When contrasted with the orientation of an Indian child and an adult, the two notions are different. Analysing the Indian mind the noted psychoanalysts Kakar and Kakar, point out that in India, high cultural value is placed on connection and relationships. They further state "The high value placed on connection does not mean that an Indian is incapable of functioning when he is by himself or that he does not have a sense of his own agency. What it does imply is his greater need for ongoing mentorship, guidance and help from others in getting through life and a greater vulnerability to feeling of helplessness when these ties are strained." (Kakar & Kakar, 2007, p.197).

If the basis of practices in the Indian situation were to be guided by the Indian attitudinal and value orientation, the practices that motivate people in America and India would be different. This is borne out by the experience of organisaional and social life. Organisations in Indian businesses which have developed an affiliative and cooperative (contrasted with competitive) stance have experienced higher trust among employees at all levels and an environment of cooperation. The examples of this are many. The TVS group in South India Eicher in North India, and Crompton Greaves in Western India are only three examples to illustrate the point. There are many other organisations that are reported in the literature on the subject. (Ahmad and Chopra, 2004; Budhiraja and Athreya, 1996; Chakraborty, 1987).

In social environment and in business, simple living, renunciation, caring are valued. Indian leaders who have followed a simple, austere and community orientation beyond self have earned public respect. Gandhi, Nehru, Maulana Azad, in Indian national life and business leaders like Lala Shri Ram, JRD Tata, Narayna Murthi and others have respect of a large number of people in the country. Refering to Sufi beliefs, Siddiqui says, "The sign of a true Sufi is that he feels poor when he has wealth, is humble when he has power and hides when he has fame" (Siddique, 2005, p, 246). People feel closer to leaders when they show such characteristics. In interviews with people over many years we have found that people share such beliefs— wealth and power that wealth brings is respected but not necessarily the individuals.

We are not suggesting a model of behaviour but wish to only highlight the differences in the primary orientation of people in two cultures. As these notions and societal values are rooted in the minds of individuals, they are likely to respect leader-behaviour which fits in with their image of people who direct their lives. These unconscious images guide the expectations of people in their environment, especially those who hold positions of authority. The orientation of the Americans and the Indians suggest that patterns of relationships that invoke positive response from people in two cultures are likely to be different. However unreal and "idealistic" these notions may appear to some readers, the 'ideals' are found in the textbooks that we read in schools. Kakar content-analysed the books that are given to children in schools and found that these features were conveyed in the books (Kakar, 1970). The attitudes and values that are imbibed by individuals who are brought up in traditional families and society are further reinforced in their school textbooks.

Even without fully accepting the differences and the imagery, it is apparent that behavioural dimensions between the Westerners and a large number of Indians who have been brought up in traditional families are influenced by concepts of man and society. It follows that these notions imbedded in the conscious or unconscious mind would influence the individual's responses in relationships in the organsiation. These attitudes and values should in substance underscore the policies, approaches, practices and relationships in the organisation. There is therefore need for management to examine these issues for developing a system that could generates pontaneous will to cooperate" among employees.

The Alternative Systems of Management

After World War II, the Japanese organisations outdid some of the largest and the most successful businesses in the Western world. In most cases Japanese trainers and practicing executives studied American practices and adapted them to suit their own traditions and culture, especially in relation to people management. These practices, as they evolved, were different in many respects than the American. Slowly the conviction grew that there are more ways than one for effective management of business. The Russian, the Korean, the Chinese and some other countries developed practices that integrated appropriately with the culture and traditions in their own society. As only a few persons in these societies were familiar with english language, some experienced persons visited the western countries but adapted the practices to suit the natural responses of people in their respective countries. Through this mechanism the characteristics of the organisational culture and that of the wider society enabled people to comfortably adjust to the work situation.

The process of knowledge transfer from the West was different in India. The managerial personnel in most cases were educated in American or European universities and in many cases worked there for a length of time. They were a product of US/ European traditions. They attempted to graft the practices prevailing in the West in the Indian educational programmes and in the work environment. The obvious result was that masses of people who interpreted the practices in their own way experienced a distance from the managers. The alien practices were discomforting and they evolved their own secret standards of relating to the environment. They developed a social organisation among themselves which excluded managers (Sheth, 1968). The supervisors followed the instructions of the higher management but in many cases either colluded with employees or became hostile to them. In some organsiations where management developed an affiliative and responsive style the cooperation and mutuality prevailed in the social system. As illustration, Sundram Fastener, Eicher, Parry, Samtel developed integrated and a trusting environment. There are many examples of organisations that succeeded in evolving a cooperative system and many who failed to do so. The first author visited a few cooperative manufacturing oranisations where employees themselves had responsibility for product quality, maintenance of equipment and output. There were no supervisors. The employees maintained quality standards and helped one another when such help was needed.

When employees are fully integrated in the work community and organisation, they are likely to experience a bond between the company and themselves, and they are more likely to work for the well-being and growth of the company. They are likely to create value for the company by developing creative application of their skills. Some guidelines to develop situation of mutual acceptance based on literature and experience are discussed below (Dayal, 2007).

The employee should not be seen as an isolated individual but as a member of the family. The social system of the company should regard family, not the individual as a unit. Some of the ways in which companies have expressed this notion are:-

i. Organising family education/training/skill or literacy classes for the family.

ii. Formally organizing visits of the members of the family to the factory to see how work is done.
iii. Involving families in groups to improve the quality of life in their community.
iv. Organise cooperatives of family members to engage in productive work.
v. Provide educational facilities for dependents of families
vi. Arrange social functions for employees and their families with top and senior management at periodic intervals. In some cases children of the employees are encouraged to arrange social programmes on such occasions.

These are some ways that are practiced by some companies but there are possibly a great many other activities to bring families closer to the organisation.

As far as possible work should be organised in identifiable groups, and avoid individual assignments. The group work and sharing responsibility among members helps in developing interacting relationships and a social group. Many examples of the arrangement are available in publications on the subject (Rice 1958; Dayal 2004; Dogra 2006).

Supervision of work has to include personal relationships, beside work related issues. The supervisors have to develop competence and skills in dealing with groups, problem-solving as against fault-finding attitude, interpersonal competence and sensitivity towards human processes.

While administrative channels for decision making are necessary to avoid chaos in the organisation, individuals should have access to anyone they feel necessary to approach to discuss their ideas or problems. Wilfred Brown refers to this arrangement as looped communication. CMC prior to take over by the present management followed this system. The Indian Institute of Management, Lucknow followed this system with great advantage. Many fresh ideas come from individuals down the line. They also developed the practice of an open house where anyone could ask questions, explanations and give suggestions. There are accounts of many organisations where such practices are followed with great effect. (Ahmad & Chopra, 2004) J. R. D. Tata encouraged this practice in Tata Steel.

The group working and urge to improve would be enhanced if the notion to compete with oneself i.e., to set goals to do better from one's own performance, is promoted rather than competition. The research data shows that processes that lead to cooperation are different from those that generate differences among people and conflict. This notion is consistent with the ethos of the Indian culture and tradition.

Implication for Family Businesses

Family owned businesses:

The discussion in this book relates primarily to medium and large family-owned and managed businesses and not small 10-20 employee organisations. About 80 to 90 per cent of all businesses worldwide are family owned. Only less than 10 per cent of these survive by the third generation. At the same time many of the largest businesses are family owned. Most Japanese and Korean conglomerates are family owned. Equally true is the demise of many large family owned businesses that dominated markets 30-40 years ago and no longer figure in the survival list. (Tripathi 1990). In India the family-owned and public sector organisations are responsible for building strong manufacturing and trading tradition. They have performed a pioneering role in providing a strong foundation for industrial development in the country.

Most family-managed businesses that we have talked to believe that they have to "professionalise" their management. Some have taken steps to do so. However, the notion of professionalisation is not clearly articulated, or they are hesitant in following through the process. As mentioned in earlier chapter, in some organisations the younger generation have acquired professional qualifications before entering business. In some others professionally qualified persons are appointed to look after operations. The question for articulation is what does professionalising management systems involve?

The growth of business depends upon entrepreneurial action. The individual sees opportunity and he or she grabs it. There is always risk involved in entrepreneurial action. The entrepreneur is able to garner resources to start a project. A family-owned business is able to command resources more easily than others, especially because in pre-liberalised era resource generation from banks was difficult. Families in many cases were able to pool their resources to foot-start business. The mental set in entrepreneurial role has strong element of risk taking and in managerial role it is caution, data-based analysis, weighing limitations etc. At present owners themselves generally perform both functions. Whether these roles are performed by the owner or a person employed as chief executive (CEO), the requirements of each role need to be understood. This is not to say that managerial role has no entrepreneurial function but lack of competence to undertake measures to build an interacting and a cooperative work arrangement is critical for this role. The manager has to organise the tasks based on the nature of work and the support systems needed for managerial effectiveness. In many organisations owner-manager functions as a proprietor and in doing so make managerial roles ineffective. The ownership in corporate structure is different from the role of a proprietor in early stages of an organisation. We have observed that often owners as CEOs function as proprietors. In this style of working the managerial structure down the line becomes weak and they have little choice except to develop a supra-manager arrangement with attendant problems along with the alternatives open to family managed businesses are discussed in the earlier chapter on family businesses.

Multinational Organisations:

Multinational organisations from abroad gain market dominance from the reputation that their home organisations have achieved globally. They also have strong backing of R&D from their home organisations. As mentioned in earlier discussion in the chapter on Multinational Organisations they achieve efficiency and compliance through financial incentives and strong reward for good work and behviour and punishment for deviant behaviour. In our interviews we found that a large number of employees felt stress and a kind of alienation for reasons discussed earlier. Some of the inbuilt organisational advantages derived from the reputation of their parent organisations may not in future be quite the same as now. The development in Indian managed organisation may catch up. The research team believes that inspite of their comparatively stronger HRD efforts, it would be useful for them to consider sociological aspects discussed in this chapter. The quantitative analysis of job satisfaction data in Chapter 6 also confirms this view.

Another aspect that many of the newer multinationals have, has to do with their pre-occupation with profits alone. They would have to look at the sociological aspects as well. The HRD practices by themselves will not serve this purpose.

The Indian multinationals in foreign lands have to either selectively apply the Indian styles of management or integrate more fully with the local ways of working. The Japanese companies located in foreign lands have tended to successfully retain their styles of working in operations abroad. The Indian multinationals would have to consciously opt for their strategies as they gain experience in managing their operations abroad. The branches of Banks and Construction projects in most countries have tended to employ ethnic population. By and large the Indian and the native population have socially moved in their respective groups. Now that Indian multinationals are beginning to increase their activities in foreign lands, the social and operational relationships would need closer attention by the organsiations concerned. The Indian managers would have to develop sensitivity for socio-cultural aspects of diverse groups and develop capability to manage diversity. The experience suggests that integrating the diverse groups is more productive than each operating in separate orbits. Inter-group research has shown that joint projects contribute more to integrating diverse groups than any other single approach (Dayal, 2002; Sherif 1967). Most organisations have found that training in managing diversity is important for developing competence in handling problems and issues involved in managing diversity.

The Public Sector Enterprises:

As a policy the Government has retained ownership of companies operating in certain sectors of the economy. We have discussed the issues relating to public sector enterprises in the earlier chapter. The Government has to seriously review the selection process of chief executives for these enterprises and substantially allow reorientation of their management practices. Alternatives are contained in reports that already exist in large numbers. Most reports indicate that the administrative ministries concerned have to redefine their involvement with the enterprises and the companies themselves have to move from a bureaucratic system of working to develop market oriented responsive styles of managing.

The Tasks Ahead

In a competitive situation organisations have to prepare themselves for certain special considerations which are essential to survive in the situation. Some of these are briefly discussed below:-

i. Creativity and innovation
ii. Managing diversity
iii. Articulation and observance in practice of the values in everyday business within the organisation. The consistency in value based behaviour give confidence to employees in management and strengthen bonds of employees with the organisation.
iv. Technology and social organisation i. e. harmonising man-machine relationship.

Creativity and innovation

Creativity in the emerging environment would be necessary in respect to the product, processes and evolving new ways of managing. It is also needed in very many other ways such as thinking about different ways of doing a job or conceptualising or defining a problem, etc. In all aspects of business operations creative ways are required to develop an efficient work organisation. For example some people think of large population as so many more mouths to feed; it can also be seen as so many more pairs of hands to help build things. The action will be vastly different depending on how one perceives and defines a problem. If one sees the problem as so many mouths to feed, the planner would primarily be concerned with how to produce more food to feed, in the case he sees the problems as two pairs of hands, he would be primarily concerned about creation of jobs and developing needed skills.

There may be notable exceptions but generally creative urge manifests through a combination of several circumstances such as the following:

- The people must have opportunity to interact openly with other people including outsiders. Recent worldwide survey by IBM of countries and organisations also highlights that for innovation, open interaction with people within and outside the organisation is necessary (IBM; 2006; Dayal, 1994).
- Individuals are encouraged to articulate ideas and experiment with them. Ideas are not shot down as irrelevant or unworkable without adequate discussion. Often an idea matures, and gets modified and refined when they are articulated or after discussion with other people who raise questions that lead to reformulation of an idea or sharpen it.
- Often some discussion on an altogether different topic generates a spark and suddenly some totally unconnected ideas which are imbedded in one's mind become clearer.

This happens when a person keeps an open mind without preconceived prejudices and works in an environment of openness in the organisation. The first author recalls a discussion with a CEO who was highly respected by everyone in the organisation. He had attended an executive programme that was conducted by the researcher. In one conversation when a particular event was quoted he suddenly said "Oh, I now understand the concept that was discussed in the programme". Often individuals connect some ideas that may have occurred to them at some time and some unrelated point gets clarified in some other discussion.This is how individuals get insights. At another time someone was explaining a point to the Late Prime Minister Rajiv Gandhi who suddenly made the point and said "I understand what I saw in the agriculture exhibition in Delhi". On another occasion one colleague who is not a physicist was visiting a project in physics department in the university. The physician was explaining the project and our colleague was asking him questions. In response to a question the physicist suddenly responded that he got an idea to follow up a certain line of investigation which might provide answer to what he was seeking. Such interactions are necessary in organisations to develop new perspectives.

- Many organisations have brain storming sessions on a regular basis to generate alternatives on certain issues and encourages exchange of ideas. The discussions help individuals to bring out ideas that may be imbedded in their minds.

Indian organisations are inclined to set out prescriptive rules and regulations in almost all aspects of work. Attempt is made to structure every aspect of work and life. Even in institutions that are set up for research and education, the rigidity imposed by supervisory and management authority generate conditions that discourage independent thinking and freedom to experimenting with ideas (Dayal, 1994; Hussain 1986,). The freedom to express and encouragement to have individuality that US institutions provide have paid rich dividends to the nation and the organisations (Burnstein, 1988). Even business organisations dealing in high technology such as AT & T, IBM, Microsoft and others deliberately create system that encourage creativity. These conditions apply to research and educational systems and also to business and administrative organisations.

Managing diversity

Companies abroad, especially in the USA are by design seeking employees from different ethnic groups, languages, backgrounds and such considerations. They have found that people with diverse backgrounds have been good for their business especially in respect to the following:

i. Enhancing quality of decision making by exploring varied responses to issues and problems and reaching consensus.
ii. Developing better understanding of diverse market environments
iii. Greater tolerance among employees
iv. Developing company image in the larger community
v. Urge among employees to do as well as other groups which constitute the diversity.

The experience also suggests that special efforts were needed by the management to manage diversity. In fact a large number of companies have employed consultants to help the company develop management practices and policies to effectively use diversity to their advantage.

India has had probably the largest number of diverse groups with their own identifiable culture, language and religion. This diversity is reflected in the employee force in most large organisations. However, the typical approach of management is to manage each diverse group the best way possible. In fact most organisations do not pay particular attention to this aspect of the employee-mix. This is perhaps due to the fact that general population itself represents diverse groups of people. In society each group develops and lives separate lives. There has been no serious attempt to manage diversity for gainful purpose. In the emerging environment of globalisation the management would have to increasingly cope with diversity. It can be an asset or a disruptive element leading to inter group miscommunication, hostility and back biting. We believe that management in India would have to pay special attention to the management of diversity to derive advantage from the perspectives that they are capable of bringing to the decision making process. This is specially required when they set up operations abroad. In this context a policy and a strategy to manage diversity is perhaps necessary.

Corporate values

Sociologically business organisations are an instrument of society. They are dependent upon society for sustenance and the society expects them to provide needed goods, services and wealth.

The employees, the customers and the suppliers, etc, bring their value system into the corporation. In turn corporations influence the values of the society, especially through employees who imbibe corporate values and transmit them to their families and the society. There is mutuality in respect to exchange of values. Eventually the values in the corporation and the society harmonise. In a traditional society such as India the value frame in the wider society and the business organsiations are different. The mutuality mentioned above helps in harmonizing the two. This phenomenon has occurred in the West and this will also happen in India. If it is desirable to preserve values, that contribute to the quality of life in India such as closeness of family ties, tolerance, spirituality, respect for elders, etc., the corporate culture would have to reflect these in their organisations. These values would be difficult to capture in social life after they are replaced by individualism, competition, etc. The West is unable to regain traditional values now inspite of the leadership's efforts to do so. The management and supervisory practices should evolve around these set of values and attitudes for emotional involvement of employees. This kind of involvement is basic to innovation and for creating hunger for knowledge. Our studies show that companies which develop practices consistent with cultural orientation of employees are able to develop productive relationships at work compared to those which impose alien values in framing policies and practices.

Harmonising man-machine relationship

The industrial revolution in the West changed the man-machine relationship. The machine acquired the skills that man had, rendering man to perform what may be called the role of an attendant to the machine. Ultimately in more recent period the robotisation has eliminated the role of man altogether. Progressively the man's work became routinised. The sociologists have referred to this as alienation—the individuals became removed from the job. The job did not involve a great deal of mental capability except in higher level occupations where man directed machine and output.

In our interviews of employees we found some interesting examples of this phenomenon. The management tried in a chemical factory to rotate employees on a conveyor belt packing line. The purpose was to reduce or minimise boredom of workers who operate continuously at only one station. However the employees resisted this move inspite of many explanations provided by the supervisor. We asked the employees why did they resist the arrangement. The standard response was that they do the job in a mechanical way and think about many personal experiences and things in their life unconnected with work. If they are shifted to another position to do some other work they will have to pay attention to the job. The workers avoided monotony in their own way. Their physical self, not the thinking self, was involved in the job. This is the example of alienation from work.

Social scientists at Tavistock Institute in London and later many others found ways of organising work in a way that the employee gains some control over work. This exercise was referred to as job enlargement. This idea has been enlarged in many different ways. The central theme is that individual involvement is related to the discretionary content of the job. By providing discretionary element in the design of work, an employee would be using his "thinking" self as well. Job design has not received enough attention of a large number of companies in India.

We believe that result orientation at each level would be difficult without re-designing jobs to ensure that operatives have scope for self-involvement(Reddin 1987).

Summing up

In this chapter we have identified some of the managerial practices that business organisations would have to develop for their own growth, and in many cases, survival. Organisations that loose their market position would find it difficult to regain that position without a massive effort. In many cases the effort requires extraordinary inputs to revive by exceptional people. IBM experience is an interesting example in this respect (Grestner, Jr., 2002), IBM was a leader in computer business but lost its business to many other companies. They had option to close down the company or regain their market position when intervention by an extraordinary leader was able to revive it. The effort required rationalisation of manpower, totally new product range, new skills and new styles of managing the company.

The Indian organisations which are acquiring companies abroad would have to develop sensitivities in the countries where they begin operations. The ideas that we have discussed in this chapter would have to receive special attention of Indian multinationals.

Approach to Reorientation

Our visit to many companies other than multinationals, suggests that preparing an organisation for global competition may need comprehensive changes in many aspects of its activities. Piecemeal changes are unlikely to give the desired results.

The experience of many large corporations confirms this phenomena. For example, Life Insurance Corporation of India (LIC) undertook a five year phased programme to transfer one by one the policy servicing from Divisional to Branch office. The purpose of this undertaking was to improve the policy servicing to policy holders. They found that this exercise merely resulted in higher cost to LIC without any noticeable difference in the quality of service to the customer. LIC had to take up a comprehensive reorgnaisation to achieve the goals they had in mind. The exercise required all aspects of working such as redesign of work, a change in administrative practices, policy making functions, redistribution of authority and power, etc. (Kumar, 1991). State Bank of India (SBI) had similar experience which, among other considerations, led to total reorganisation of the Bank (Das, 1971). The literature provides many examples of the kind mentioned here (Gestner, 2002; De, 1984). The rationale for this phenomena is provided in open systems theory or concept (Miller and Rice, 1967). In a highly simplified expression, an organisation is comparable to human body. Any dysfunctionality in one sub-system, say nervous system would show up in the digestive or the respiratory sub-system. In good health all five sub-systems are in a state of balance. Imbalance in one sub-system affects other sub-systems because all of these are inter-dependent. In the same manner any change in one department or function in an organisation could cause imbalance or disruptions in other functions. Many Japanese organisations follow a very simple procedure in this respect. When one department wants to change some work practice they write it up and circulate it to all other departments to study what changes they would have to make in their procedures to avoid any disconnection. Once the matters has been studied by concerned people the changes in all departments are brought about simultaneously.

According to our observations, research and consulting experiences the reorientation in many organisations would have to be comprehensive to be able to compete in global environment. The nature of new challenges are outlined in chapter 1. Many of the existing organisations have a long history of success. To remain successful in the emerging environment and to face the nature of market challenges that organisations would progressively face require serious consideration.

Past achievements do not guarantee continuing success. In fact in many cases success has inbuilt seeds of failure. Some years ago we had been invited by a very large Indian conglomerate to suggest how their success can be sustained in future. We studied many aspects of their working and met senior managers individually and in groups. To almost every suggestion the response was that the organisation has successfully done things in certain ways and there was no need to change the practice. No change in product modification, marketing approach or management practices was possible except a few minor changes at the CEO level. Eventually we decided with mutual consent to withdraw from the assignment. In about 15 years the organisation gradually lost its business and it no longer exists now. Organisational change requires time investment by the top and senior management and patience to work through problem areas.

People Development (HRD related)

Human Resource Development (HRD) foundation in many organisations have drawn attention to human aspect of management. Interventions initiated by HRD have developed practices that have considerably enhanced the contribution of people in the organisation (Dayal et al, 1996). We believe that in many organisations the orientation of HRD practices would have to shift. Broadly, a number of programmes predominantly aim at what Herzberg has called hygiene factors (Rao 1997; Silvera, 1988). These are important but people development has to evolve around what Herzberg has identified as motivating factors. We believe that organisations would have to seriously consider the many aspects that concern sociology of work orgnaisations. These aspects have been discussed earlier.

A related issue that needs emphasis is briefly discussed here. It has to do with the leadership that growth organisations require for developing human systems, especially the aspect of people development.

Positive Leader Behaviour

In a situation where cooperation of people and a spirit of working together is required the leader behaviour would have to be primarily concerned with encouraging people to think and develop ideas. Leader would need to help people gain confidence in themselves. He or she would have to be perceptive enough to recognise strengths and weaknesses of people, and develop realistic plan to achieve observable results (Adair, 2003).

All socio-psychological studies such as David McClelland's and Hofstede and our own show that Indians have strong power needs – automatic inclination to control people and situations.

The researchers believe that the leader would need affiliative and achievement orientation and those who are strong in these characteristics are likely to contribute to a high achieving organisation. The management advisors have developed effective intervention strategies to help people change their need orientation. There is strong evidence that people with power-orientation may succeed in driving an organisation to reach great heights of achievement, but such organisations often fail to keep the momentum soon after they depart.

Reorienting Organisation

In taking up a serious exercise to reorient the organisation, it is necessary to recognize that the top and senior management have contributed to whatever is the state of the organisation. While undertaking a massive exercise to reorient the Steel Authority of India (SAIL) the then Chairman, Mr V Krishnamurti held off-site meeting with senior management personnel and posed a question to them "What have we as management contributed to the organisation for its being what it is now." (the statement expresses the sentiment, not the words). The Chairman encouraged people to discuss the role of the management without becoming defensive about their behaviour. This question led to examination of the overall situation over the two days of the meeting. This interaction followed many such meetings down the line including about 250000 employees. SAIL helped employees to identity problems and in many cases find solutions. At the end of the intensive exercise for changing culture of the organisation, SAIL was able to show impressive improvements. The various stages of the programme have been documented by SAIL. There are some independent studies of the exercise on transforming one of the largest corporations in the country (Dayal and Aggarwal, 1995).

Crompton Greaves was rated high among the successful technology based organisations. In 1985 the new CEO, Mr KK Nohria found that the company was in bad trim. He wrote in his book that "the wind had abruptly changed direction, catching the management unawares. It was my job primarily to set the sails right again and correct the course" (Nohoria, 1998 p.1) The book describes in detail the programme undertaken by the organisation to transform itself and to regain its position. The main features of the programme in brief are:

i. Basically all organisational tasks were reoriented with focus on customer, employees, quality of product and service, productivity, cost and sharing and learning

ii. the strategy involved, as in SAIL, discussion and consensus at the top levels of management, and at all levels down to the workers. All these efforts simultaneously included training, improving systems and competence building. The management worked on the basis that employees strive for self improvement and "where they fail to deliver desired results, faulty process and not persons" are likely to be responsible. It is therefore better to improve the process rather than blame the person. Continuous attention was paid to the processes which were reengineered and improved until they were secure, waste-free, defect-free and accident-free.

iii. Constant attention was given at all levels to ethical issues and these were clearly articulated and reviewed.

The organisation achieved concrete results between 1985 to 1996:

- Sales ranking of the company improved from 43 to 23.
- The company expanded its product base in its existing portfolio and also successfully diversified into Industrial Controls, Telecommunication and Informatics.
- From five plants mainly in Maharashtra to additional plants spread all over India.
- Consistent improvement in productivity and the financial parameters.

There are many organisations in India which have undertaken impressive reorientation of their business and organisations. However, in every known situation deep involvement of the CEO and the senior persons in the organisation is necessary and the programme includes all key aspects of its work. This was also the case in LIC and SBI, reported earlier in the book.

The programme details are taken from the book by K. K. Noharia to highlight the approach of reorienting the organisation.

Chapter 8

Survey of Literature

This chapter examines the literature on management styles in three kinds of organisations – family managed, multinationals and public sector enterprises in India

Family Managed Enterprises

Management practices, to a large extent, reflect the values and belief systems, which have been the cradle of decision makers as they were growing up. This is, more true in traditional societies in general and family owned organisations in particular.

Families are social institutions that have evolved in human societies from producing individuals capable of perpetuating societies (Waterman, 2003). Most parents seek to help their children become competent adolescents by initialising them into the norms and values of family and larger society. Since families are important in developing and maintaining values, linkage between work and family are important to organisations (Carlson and Kocmar, 2000). Work environment includes such variables as interpersonal relations, supervision, work pressure, autonomy, job orientation and other socially contrived factors. Hence the cluster pattern organisationally desired outcomes are based on the family values that are inculcated in the process of socialisation in the family and the community.

There is sufficient evidence to suggest that Indian managers in family owned organisations and managers in other traditional and non-traditional societies avoid doing things that may reflect poorly on family and social milieu to which they belong.

Based on his research, Pareek (1988) concludes that organisations must make sure that such positive qualities such as concern for others, tendency to harmonise and synthesise various point of views should be taken into consideration while designing and managing organisations. In a case study developed by Gandhi and Saiyadain (2003) on the management style of Managing Director of Atlas Cycles (family owned organisation) found that a large number of family values got reflected in his management practices. Respect for elders still prevailed in the organisation. Since nothing was done under the table, the cost of cycles were higher than their competitors. Family was docile and close knit and decision making was conservative and playing safe was the norm.

In a study of Turkish employees, Katrinli *et al* (2006) collected data from 149 employees and asked them to list 10 different values that are supposed to be dominant in their natal family life. Based on the ratings of judges, 21 values were found to be most dominant (sharing, commitment, love, respect, trust, democracy, self sacrifice, tolerance, freedom, high value to people, consistency, responsibility, harmony, equality, honesty, conservatism, philanthropy, justice, hard work, materialism and peace). In the second phase of the study, 176 Turkish employees rated these values on a 3-point scale indicating their degree of existence in their family life and work conditions. The results showed a high degree of congruence between family and work values.

In another case study of Kamla Dials and Devises Limited, Gandhi and Saiyadain (2003a) identified the concept of "significant others" playing a major role in decision making. These significant others were the elder members of the family and the senior, more experienced people whose opinions were respected because respect for elders was ingrained in the mind of managing director.

Based on his long years of experience and research, Dayal (1977) suggested that in most organisations work appears to generate dependence on superiors and emphasis on formal roles rather than close informal relationships. This he found contrary to personalised relationship, exercise of authority based on affiliative concerns and having a father figure. Sinha (1980) in his leadership studies found that many successful companies showed care for subordinates, showed affection, took personal interest in their well-being and commitment to the personal growth of the employees. He called this as Nurturing Leadership Style.

In a profile write-up of Sir Anthony Banford, McCulloch (2002) talks about—like father like son syndrome. Joseph Cyril Banford (JCB) an engineering company founded in 1945 by his father and named after him, grew from a small organisation at inception to a large organisation now. When Sir Anthony (the son) took over its management two principles which were followed by his father, hard work and delegation became his mantra. Today these two concepts have become the work ethics of JCB.

Gupta (1993) while comparing American, Japanese and Indian workers concluded that while the Americans are individualistic and draw meaning from their work, and the Japanese workers feel that they belong to their work organisation, the Indian workers draw meaning largely from their familial values and relationships. Chakraborty (1987 and 1988) goes a step beyond and suggests that management styles of Indian managers should be seen in the light of religious adherence. He suggests that ***guna*** theory of ***samkhya*** could be more appropriate model in the Indian context.

Multinational Enterprises

Globalisation has brought about a process of convergence and assimilation of social, cultural and political aspects of life. Multinational organisations (MNC) that have crossed the boundaries of home country to do business in host countries are more susceptible to the process of convergence and assimilation. Practices rooted in local idiosyncrasies may appear complex but have to be recognised, appreciated and accepted if MNCs have to survive in host countries. Country of origin effects can be strenghtened if nationals from the home country are hired and if local administrative preferences are embedded in the structures and design of MNCs (Noorderhaven and Harzing, 2003).

Bartlett and Ghoshal (1992) suggested that in order to survive in home country, MNCs have to pursue three different but complementary objectives. The first is *local responsiveness*: MNCs should undertake an exhaustive survey of the markets and suite their products to fit the preferences of their clients. The second objective is *global integration:* MNCs' operations should take advantage of different national factors of production. The third objective is to develop *innovation and learning organisation* which requires that different units learn from each other and exchange innovations in management systems and processes. Bonache *et al* (2001) argue that to be able to achieve these objectives two things must be done— (i) selection of managers in home country, for host country should focus on the degree to which the individual has internalised the corporate values so that these managers are "trustworthy". (ii) subsidiary managers should be sent to home country so as to train them in the values and ways of working the organisation.

In the following pages four research studies from four different countries/region have been examined. These studies highlight the management styles of MNCs and how they have adopted to local values and culture.

In a study in Greece, Myloni *et al* (2004) examined the human resource management practices by MNCs and their local subsidiaries. Using data collected from MNCs, subsidiaries located in Greece and local Greek firms the authors studied the similarities in human resource practices. Their results showed that subsidiaries have adopted from parent organisation their HRM practices to a considerable extent, though some of the practices were found to be more localised than others. Those practices, which were not consistent with Greek culture or in contrast to employee regulations showed a low level of transfer. However the authors also noted that the institutional environment in Greece was getting more relaxed giving more room to MNCs.

In another study of Chinese MNCs operating in United Kingdom, Zhang and Edwards (2003) studied the natural differences that influenced the HRM choices and practices of the subsidiaries and the influence of change in Chinese business systems since 1980 when these companies started their international expansion. Their results highlighted three major conclusions. First, they found that strategy choices are shaped by the need to compete in the international market. Secondly, the scope and extent of localisation reflected the characteristics of the stage of development of the country of origin. Thirdly, the process of localisation reflected the characteristics of Chinese business system. Specifically, control and top down process gave managers in subsidiaries little decision making autonomy.

Control and top down approach was also reported by Rosten (1991). Power in Russian organisations rests in the hands of General Director with little influence on the decision making process by middle management. The hierarchical, centralised and utilitarian nature of business decisions implies that the vision of the person can dramatically influence business orientation. Hence those General Directors who could recognise economic forces like inflation and competition may adopt the home practices much more easily. They may be quick to re-structure and develop more competitive strategies, increase promotion and sales force and seek foreign investment (Shama, 1994).

In a futuristic paper on Asia-Pacific region Fujimoto and Hartel (2006) developed a module to the effect of individualistic-collectivistic interaction (ICI) within the organisation. They suggested that the outcome of ICI is mediated by inter group prejudice of the collectivists and the interpersonal prejudice of the individual. As a result of globalisation the work force will become culturally diverse and MNCs operating in Asia-Pacific region would have to adjust this diversity.

From these studies what seems to emerge is that MNC practices are more prone to local cultural influence than their over all practices and strategies. Tayeb (1998) suggests that we need to make a distinction between policies and practices. Using findings of a case study of an American company in Scotland he argues that organisations might find it feasible to have company wide policies, they might find it unavoidable to be responsive to local conditions when it comes to practices. He further argues that some practices can be transferred across nations without change, some must be modified to become workable and some are so culture specific that they cannot be transferred.

Public Sector Enterprises

It is generally believed that most public sector undertakings (PSUs) have not been very effective. Mishra (2006) believes that some of the reasons for poor performance by PSUs can be found in the very structure of PSUs. Public Enterprise Selection Board takes long time in identifying and placing the top management in positions. Their salaries and benefits are not competitive vis-à-vis those in private sector and they have limited autonomy in terms of decision making. In fact their performance is constrained by a large number of factors very often outside the very structure of PSUs. This point is further elaborated in an essay by Vernon (1990). While managers in PSUs have demanded and received special privileges and subsidised resources to support their commercial activities, the Government (read Ministers) have also demanded responsiveness and accountability. One such attempt has been the creation of ministries for state owned enterprises. Given more or less the same conditions some other PSUs have shown profit and effectiveness. Research evidence on the managerial styles of PSU managers throws some light on this dilemma.

In a study of leadership effectiveness in PSU managers, Mathew (2006) developed a leader-relations model. After examining leadership effectiveness in terms of empowerment, emotional intelligence and structural implications he came to the conclusion that leader-relations model overcomes the defects of classical model. It forms relational areas links to attempts so as to alleviate the negative effects of task concerns and to bring forward the positive effect on relational concerns.

Most studies on the management styles of PSU managers have been comparative in nature. In other words, their style of management has been seen in the context of the managerial styles of managers in the private sector. In one such comparative framework, Agarwal and Bose (2004) examined the effectiveness of PSU mangers. Their sample consisted of 105 managers belonging to two public sector undertakings and 100 managers from two private sector organisations. The study was aimed to identify aspects of organisational work climate that may contribute to perception of procedural justice in the two sectors. Organisational work climate was indexed in terms of climate of innovation, level of interpersonal trust, participative decision making and member welfare. High scores on these four variables correlated significantly with the perception of procedural justice more so for managers in PSUs than their counterparts in private sector. What these results imply is that PSU managers who practice innovative climate, interpersonal trust, joint decision making and member welfare were perceived to show fairness in human resource practices.

Yet some other studies suggest somewhat different results. Using questionnaire and interview data, Verma (2006) developed a nine point grid module based on two dimensions – concern for personnel policies and rules and concern for people. These two dimensions led to five combinations ranging from 1 to 9. He called them routine (1.1), paternalistic and friendly (1.9), custodian of rules and policies (9.1), creativity and problem solving (9.9) and compromising (5.5). The results showed that of the two PSUs, organization As management, instead of looking ahead for engaging in problem solving or anticipatory management, were busy with trivial day to day matters with little inclination to delegate and take decisions based on consistent management practices (a 1.1 position). The managers in organisation felt that they have lost their power to extract work from employees for fear of physical assault. Instead all work was done by pampering and personal influence (a 1.9 position).

Based on a number of case studies, it was observed that in defining their goals and objectives PSUs are influenced more by values than by economic aspects (Murthy, 1988). Values refer to personal values of key decision makers, their desires and preferences and their conception of ideal. Economic aspects refer to consideration such as product, cost and markets etc. This seems to be more true in the old PSUs as compared to the new.

A study by Mishra and Rath (1988) found that aspects of quality of work life were much better in the old PSUs as compared to the new PSUs. Using this line of thought Pattanayak *et al* (2005) conducted a study of four hundred employees from four PSUs (100 from each of them). These four were Rourkela Steel Plant (established in 1959), Hindustan Aeronautic Limited (established in 1965), National Thermal Power Corporation (established in 1975) and National Aluminium Company (established in 1981). Two significant results were found. Executives of old PSUs used more of nurturant as well as bureaucratic style of leadership, while executives of new PSUs used more authoritarian and task oriented style. Secondly, executives of new PSUs used reward and expert power while their counterparts in old PSUs used referent power.

Bagaram Tulpule, noted trade unionist and General Manager Durgapur Steel Plant summarised the changing profile of PSU managers (1977). The stereotypical profile of managers in PSUs as bureaucratic, aloof, impersonal and non-committed to enterprise which he heads has changed. The present manager of PSU does not conform very much to the concurrent thinking and is reasonably result oriented.

References

Adair, John (2003), *The Inspirational Leader: How to Motivate, Encourage & Achieve Success,* Kogan Page, London.

Agarwal, M and Bose, S (2004), *Organizational Climate for Perception of Procedural Fairness in Human Resource Practices and Role Efficacy*. Indian Journal of Industrial Relations, 40(2), 176-196.

Ahmad, Abad & Chopra, DP (2004), Passion to Win, Excell Book, New Delhi.

Bartlett, C and Ghoushal, S (1992), *Managing Across Borders: The Transitional Solution.* London: Century Business.

Bernstein, J (1988), T*hree Degrees Above Zero, Bell Lades in the Information Age,* Affiliated East-West Press, New Delhi.

Bonache, J, Brewster, C and Suutari, V (2001), *Expatriation: Developing Research Agenda.* Thunderbird International Business Review, 43(1), 3-20.

Brown W and Jaques, E (1965), On Glacier Project Papers, Heinemann, London.

Brown, W (1960), Piecework Abandoned, Heinemann, London.

Budhiraja, SB and Athrey, MB (El.) (1996), Cases in Strategic Management, Tata McGraw-Hill Publishing Co. Ltd. New Delhi.

Baumgartel, H, Bennis, WG and De NR, Asia, I (1967), Organisation of Work, in Reading from Group Development, Mumbai.

Chakroborty, SK (1987), Managerial Effectiveness and Quality of Work Life: Indian Insight. New Delhi: Tata McGraw Hill.

Chakroborty, SK (1988), Foundations of Managerial Work: Contributions from Indian Thought. Bombay: Himalya Publications.

Carlson, DS and Kocmar, KM (2000), Work – Family Conflict in the Organizations: Do Life Role Values Make a Difference. Journal of Management, 26(5), 1031-1055.

Das, TK (1971), Organisation in State Bank of India, Lok Udyog, New Delhi.

Dayal, I (1977), Change in Work Organisaton, New Delhi: Concept Publication.

Dayal, I and Thomas, JM (1968), Operation K P E: Developing a New Organsiation, *Journal of Applied Behavioural Science,* Vol. 4, Number 4 (Oct.-Nov.) pp 472-506.

Dayal, I (2002), Intergroups Relations: Conflict & Cooperation, *Indian Journal of Industrial Relations,* Vol. 37, New Delhi.

Dayal, I et al (1996), Successful Applications of HRD, Case Studies of Indian Organsiations, Mittal Publication, New Delhi.

Dayal, I (2007), Indianising Indian Management: A Framework, Indian Journal of Industrial Relations, July 2007.

Dayal I and Aggarwal V (1995), Modernising Organisations, New Concepts, New Delhi.

De, NR (1984), Alternative Design of Human Organisation, Sage, New Delhi.

Dogra, D. (2006), Ishwar Dayal on Management, Vol-3, Ane Books India, New Delhi.

Fujimoto, Y and Hartel, CEJ (2006), A Self Representation Analysis of the Effect of Individualistic-Collectivistic Interactions within Organizations in Individualistic Culture. *Cross Cultural Management: An International Journal,* 13(3), 204-218.

Gupta, RK (1993), Challenges in Developing Indigenous Theories of Organizations and Management. Working Paper Series WPS (2) Lucknow: Indian Institute of Management.

Gandhi, M and Saiyadain, MS (2003), Management Styles of Family Managed Organization: Case of Atlas Cycles. New Delhi: Fortune Institute of International Business.

Gandhi, M and Saiyadain, MS (2003a), Management Style in Family Managed Organization: Case of Kamla Dials and Devices Limited. New Delhi; Fortune Institute of International Business.

Grestner, Jr LV (2002), Who Says Elephants Can't Dance, Harper, New York.

Herzberg, F (1966), Work and the Nature of Man, World Publishing, Cleveland.

Hofstede, G (1980), Culture Consequences: International Differences in Work Related Values; Beverly Hills, Calif. Sage.

Hoppock, R (1935), Job Satisfaction. New York: Harper.

Hussain, A Review Committee of CSIR, Govt. of India, 1986.

Jain, R (2006), Chains that Liberates, Governance of Family firms, Macmillan, New Delhi.

Kakar, S (1971), The theme of Authority in Social Relations in India, *The Journal of Social Psychology,* 84, pp 93-101.

Kakar, S (1976), the Inner World: A Psycho-Analytic Study of Childhood and Society in India, Oxford Univ. Press, New Delhi.

Kakar S and Kakar K (2007), The Indians, Portrait of a People, Penguin, New Delhi.

Kanungo, RN (1992), Alienation and Empowerment, Same Ethical Imperative in Business *Journal of Business Ethics*, 23(1),25-29.

Katrinli, AE, Atabay, G and Gunay, G (2006), Congruence of Family and Organisational Values in Relational to Organizational Citizenship Behaviour. *Journal of Human Values*, 12:1, Kogan Page, London. 2006, pp. 81-88.

Kumar, Dharmendra (Complier) 1991), Tryst with Trust, The LIC Story, Life Insurance Corporation of India, Mumbai.

Mathews, J (2006), Leader Relations Model: Alternative Approach to Traditional Process of Leadership. *VISION Journal of Business Perspective*, 10 (4), 37-48.

McCulloch, S Playing the Long Game, Interview with Sir Anthony Branford in *Family in Business,* Sept./Oct. 2004, pp 22-25.

Miller EJ & Rice, AK (1967), Systems of Organisation, Tavistock, London.

Mishra, RK (2006), Performance of Public Enterprises in the Era of Economic Liberalization. *Journal of Institute of Public Enterprise*, 29(1&2), 1-23.

Mishra, PK and Rath, D (1988), Quality of Work Life in Old and New Organizations. Unpublished Thesis. Bhuaneshwar: Utkal University.

Murthy, KRS (1982), Strategic Management of Public Enterprise: A framework for Analysis. Working Paper. Ahmedabad: Indian Institute of Management.

Mumford, E (1991), Job satisfaction: A method of analysis. *Personal Review*, 20(3), 11-19.

Myloni, B Harzing, A and Mirza, H (2004), Host Country Specific Factors and the Transfer of Human Resource Management Practices in the Multi National Companies. *International Journal of Manpower*, 25 (60), 518-534.

Nicholson, N Reported in an Interview by Suman Nayak in Hindustan Times, October 30, 2005.

Nohria, K (1999), Painless Transition, MacMillan India Ltd., New Delhi.

Noorderhaven, NG and Herzing, A (2003), The Country of Origin Effect in Multi National Corporations: Sources, Mechanisms and Moderating Conditions. *Management International Review*, 43(2), 47-66.

Pareek, U (1988), Organizational Behaviour Process. Jaipur: Rawat Publications.

Pattanayak, B, Niranjan, P and Ganguly, S (2005), Power Dynamics, Leadership and Integration: A Study of Indian Public Sector. *International Journal of Human Resource Development and Management*, 5(1), 57-68.

Rao, TV (1997), Human Resource Development, Experiences, Interventions, Strategies, Sage, New Delhi.

Reddin, WJ (1987), Effective Management, Tata-McGraw-Hill Publishing Co. Ltd., New Delhi.

Rice AK (1958), Productivity and Social Organisation, Tavistock, London.

Rice, AK (1963), Enterprise and its Environment, Tavistock, London.

Rosten, K (1991), Soviet-US Joint Ventures: Pioneers on a New Frontier. *California Management Review*, 33(2), 88-108.

Shama, A (1994), Transformation of Marketing Management in Russia: A Qualitative and Theory Building Approach. *International Executive*, 36(5), 599-624.

Sheth, NR (1963), Informal Bonds of Factory Workers, *Economic Weekly,* Feb., 1963.

Sheth, NR (1963), Social Framework of an Indian Factory, Oxford University Press, New Delhi.

Sherif M (1967), Group Conflict and Cooperation, Routledge and Kegan Paul, London.

Siddiqui, M (2005), Corporate Soul, the Monk Writing the Manager, Response Books, New Delhi.

Silvera, DM (1986), Human Resource Development: the Indian Experience, New India Publications, New Delhi.

Singh, NK (1999), Eastern and Cross Cultural Management, Har-Anand Publications Ltd., New Delhi: Naroda Mills Case in Case Series Developed by Indian Institute of Management, Ahemedabad.

Sinha, JBP (1980), Nurturant Task Leader: A Model of the Effective Executive. New Delhi: Concept Publications.

Sinha, JBP (2000), Work Culture in Indian Context, New Delhi Sage.

Sinha JBP (2000), Basic Research Report, Managing Cultural Diversity for Productivity – The Asian Ways, Asian Productivity Organisation, Tokyo, Japan.

Tandon, PL (1971), Beyord Punjab, Thomson Press, New Delhi.

Tayeb, M (1998), Transfer of HRM practices across cultures: An American company in Scotland. *The International Journal of Human Resource Management,* 9(2), 332-358.

Tripathi, D (1990), Business Houses in Western India, Manohar Publications, New Delhi.

Tulpule, B (1977), Amidst Heat and Noise: Durgapur Recalled. New Delhi: All India Management Association.

Vaid, KN (1969), Papers on Absenteeism, Shri Ram Centre for Industrial Relations and Human Resource, New Delhi.

Verma, P (2006), Integrating Productivity with Employee Satisfaction: A Case of Two Public Sector Companies. *Indian Journal of Training and Development,* 34(4), 119-131.

Verma, YV (2006), Passion, Untold Story of LG, Biztantra New Delhi.

Vernon, R (1990), Linking Managers with Ministers: Dilemma of State Owned Enterprises. In Prajapati Trivedi (Ed) *Memorandum of Understanding: An Approach to Improving Public Enterprise Performance*. New Delhi: International Management Publishers.

Waterman, AMC (2003), Economics, Love and Family Values. *Independent Review,* 3(7), 443-454.

Wanous, JP and Lawler, EE (1972), Measurement and Meaning of Job Satisfaction. *Journal of Applied Psychology* 56,95-105.

Zhang, M and Edwards, C (2003), HRM Practices and the Influence of Country of Origin Chinese MNCs Operating in UK Paper Presented in 13th World Congress, Berlin, September 9-12.

Case Studies

Annexures : Case Study -I

Kamla Dials & Devices Ltd.

Kamla Dials and Devices ltd. (KDDL) was established in 1983 with technical collaboration from Leschot SA of Switzerland. The company was founded by Mr. Y. Sahoo as part Business Group. KDDL manufacturs watch dials and watch hands and have the distinction of being the only Indian watch component manufacturing company. Its annual production capacity is 10 million dials. In 1997 company commenced production of watch hands and today it produces 30 million hands annually. The company is the premier vendor of Titan, India's largest manufacturers of watches. It has the following units in India.

i. Dials factory at Parwanoo (HP) produces 1.2 million dials per annum. The main market is high quality European watch brands.

ii. Dials factory at Derabasi has a capital of 6.5 million dials per annum. Its main market is Indian brands and economical dials for European brands.

iii. Dials factory at Bangalore produces 3.5 million dials exclusively for Indian leading customers.

iv. Hands factory at Bangalore produces 30 million hands per annum for clients in India, Europe and Hongkong.

v. Tool Room at Bangalore makes precision blanking tools and components for industrial and medical instruments as well as for cameras.

vi. Himachal Fine Banks Ltd., manufacturs appliqué figures for watch dials.

vii. Kamla Packaging makes packaging boxes for watch and jewellery items.

In addition, it also has an export office in Hongkong. More recently (Jan 2003) KDDL has entered in retail business by opening its flagship store for premium watches in Chandigarh. Called by the name Ethos, it is the largest and the first of its kind in India and stocks more than 15 premium brands of watches including Tag Heuer, Swarovski, Rado, Omega Longiness, Swatch and Dunhill. The projection is to have 15 such stores by year 2005.

In the fiscal year 2002-2003 its turnover was 420 millions, paid up capital was Rs. 59.36 million and accumulated reserve of Rs. 193.46 million. It is a public company, listed on Bombay stock exchange with more than 5000 shareholders. The directors hold 40% of its shares.

The management believes in quest for excellence, teamwork and oneness. The corporate philosophy is based on quality, efficiency, self-development, teamwork and fairness.

Profile of Managing Director

An entrepreneur with a vision of doing things ahead of others and taking strategic steps before others was born in 1958 in the Sahoo Family. The elder of the two brothers, he did his schooling from St. Johns, High School, graduation in, Delhi University Eco (Hons.) from St. Stephens and an MBA from IIM, Ahmedabad. Married in 1982, he has two children – a daughter who is a student of economics at St. Stephens College and a son who is now in high school. His wife is a part time director in the Company owned retail outlet called Ethos.

Managing Director's business accumanship has been greatly influenced by the thinking of three persons – his father, maternal grandfather and a Chinese gentleman whom he met through the Taiwanese collaboration of KDDL. His father, as he says laid a very high insistence on quality. He was known to be an exacting person, who would pick up one thing and go into the details. If he had a bigger and better thing in his mind, he won't bother about the small things, but he was very particular about values and would do nothing was not conform that did with law.

The Chinese gentlemen taught him a lot about doing business. He used to say that "everything is in your control so don't blame anybody else". This has been a very important learning Managing Director. Who has single-mindedly followed the advice throughout his life?

Soon after his education form IIM Ahmedabad he joined his fathers business of making hosiery machine needles, which was a joint venture with a German firm. However soon he got uninterested in this business and found the product to be "damn boring with very few degrees of freedom". This he found was not something that he wanted to do and was on a lookout for a project where he did not have "to mess with messing things". Several projects were explored and finally making dials was found to be exciting. Hence Kamla Dials and Devices Limited (KDDL) came into being. This is the company in India that supplies dials and other watch components to Swiss companies. KDDL created an island of existence.

Hosiery needles, being and industrial product were 3-4 steps away from the customers, while dials are one step away from the customer. Watches were something, which he found interesting, and the high precision needed in manufacturing watch dials supported his admiration for the German ways of working. One of his long time close associates described him as an intelligent, down to earth person who is a good listener with lots of patience.

What excited him about watch dials was an infinitely larger element of design. "Watch is an interesting product and dials define the watch. Dials can be of wide variety depending on design, fashion, branding and even the preferences of individuals and watch making companies".

Growth of Business

The first dial-manufacturing factory was set up at Parwanoo, Himachal Pradesh to supply dials to Hindustan Machine Tools (HMT). By the time Parwanoo plant came up, Mr. N.D. Tiwari, the Chief Minister told HMT to put up a plant in Rani Bagh, his constituency and manufacture dials. The Chairman of HMT asked Managing Director to shift the factory to Rani Bagh. Since that was not possible, HMT would not buy from KDDL. From 1983 when the KDDL plant was set up in Parwanoo until 1987, KDDL went through a very tough time. But KDDL decided not to do anything outside the books. By 1987, KDDL had lost twice the paid up Capital.

The unit at Parwanoo was set up with Swiss technical collaboration. But by 1987, the Swiss industry had also started declining which added to the losses. This was followed by a collaboration with a Taiwanese firm, and later when Titan came in a as client in 1988, KDDL began to write off their losses as business started picking up. In 1991 KDDL set up another unit at Bangalore. This unit faced tremendous competition by a dial-manufacturing unit, which was being set up in Bangalore with Japanese collaboration and market news, was that senior managers of Titan privately supported this unit. This unit was going to be a big threat to KDDL. Moreover this was also a time when Managing Director's father was abroad on a social mission of Rotary International, as its President and so Managing Director also had to look after his father's business. Despite all odds, KDDL had to counter this threat, so it took a place on lease and started operations in Bangalore and in 6 months they made the place operational. This happened before the proposed JV at Bangalore about 25% lower than the Japanese JV company. Two years they faced competition Japanese JV from but KDDL won over them. By the end of 1997 Japanese JV collapsed. It still remains non-functional.

A third unit was set up at Derabassi, Punjab in 1997, which manufactures low end dials for Europe and high end dials for Hongkong. Parwanoo factory is for high end European market where quality and subjectivity are important. Bangalore factory essentially supplies dials to Titan where cost and quality compliance are major considerations.

Dial making is a very serious business. There is tremendous performance pressure because of market demands. Market variability is high, delivery compliances are difficult to maintain and competition is increasing. Keeping up with fashion consciousness is difficult. Technology of dial making is partly manual and quality assurance is absolutely important.

KDDL supplies 80% of Titan dial requirements, which accounts for 50% of its business. Another 35% of its turnover comes from export of which 95% are exported to Switzerland. A firm called Taratech has been set up in Switzerland to handle export. Parwanoo unit supplies dials to Rado and hopes to extend this to Omega in the next ten years. KDDL also has 2 Swiss and 2 Indian designers as consultants for unweiling new collections at 3 important fairs internationally. Today the total turnover is about 4 crores aimis to raise it to 5 crores in the near future.

Managing Director never had a great passion for marketing. So he kept a low profile and never advertised. "We never manipulated the market. We could not exaggerate the value and then let it go. We believe that value must show itself. We never did anything under the table and would not do so in future".

Ethos – Passion For Time

First of its kind, premium watch store called Ethos—Passion for Time, was set up recently to open doors for developing relations with international watch dealers. Ethos sells foreign and very expensive watches like Rolex, Rado, Calvin Klien, Nina Ricci, Tissot etc., along with Titan. The concept is to wall mount the premium watches with price tags for customers to take decisions according to the price they have in mind: It is meant for economically well-off people for whom a watch is a status symbol. Managing Director believed that retailing is happening in the world and India should not be left behind. "Ethos was a baby for which Managing Director had great passion". Being a new concept none including Managing Director had a clear idea of what shape Ethos would take. At the time of setting up Ethos margins and expenditures were not known. One crore was spent in the central office at Chandigarh, and about 12 lakhs were spent on developing software. Another 1 crore is expected to be spent in the next year. Estimates are that it would take atleast four years to break even. The plan is to open branches in Bangalore, Ludhiana and Bombay and by the end of 2005 it would be a chain of 15 store spread across the country. "Ethos stands for authenticity and value".

Employee Concerns

Interaction with staff members revealed the following concerns of the employees.

i. Quality is very important to meet the demands of international market. Being a fashion market the competition is high ad by the time the design of a particular product is ready it becomes obsolete in the market. At the same time technology is also changing very fast. What is needed is training and exposure to the latest trends and training in soft skills to the management cadre. A beginning has been made recently. Selected staff has been sent to Switzerland to visit Swiss factories and to learn the changing pattern of fashion and technology. However the process is slow and doesn't encompass a large number of employees.

ii. The top management seems to be restless. Too many changes in policies are made very frequently which hurts employees at the lower levels. As an example grades and designation are revised now and then. Employees are not clear about their future both in terms of salary structure and growth possibilities. There seems to be a general feeling of stagnation.

iii. Aesthetic and quality demands acquire urgency in decision making and action. Knowledge base in this business is changing very fast. Delivery time is too short and this becomes an obstacle in meeting quality requirements. There are major time scheduling problems because of short notice orders. Besides, location disadvantages lead to logistic problems as it takes time to get the needed component and parts for designing something new. Many a times components ordered from outside have high rejection rate which further adds to time pressure. Newer designs take a lot of time and often the time spent in designing goes waste because the customers do not find them acceptable. This creates high degree of frustration and a sense of waste. And over and above that repeat orders also do not come.

iv. Though decision-making is participative and to a large extent things are decentralised at the unit level, the behavior of management suffers on account of professional touch. A degree of impersonelisaiton has crept into the system. Units are profit centers and result oriented but they have to remind the top management about their existence, to come and visit the unit.

v. A deliberate attempt has to be made to retain the talented people. Salary structure should be revised now and then and latest technology should be incorporated. The general commitment to work seems to be low because efforts are not appropriately rewarded and a sense of belongingness needs to be developed. There is a definite need to reinforce the mission, which says "Quality is our job, Customer satisfaction is our duty and customer loyalty is our future".

vi. However by and large employees experience a high degree of mental satisfaction. This is contributed mainly by the working environment, family like atmosphere and work culture. One gets the feeling that if mistakes are made a change is given. Work is not dirty.

vii. Their major sources of irritation are, no tea is served to the workers, half as hour given for lunch has to be compensated by extra half an hour of work, overtime money is not paid instead a day off is given according to company's convenience. The workers feel that "they work hard but only the staff gets the benefits". KDDL does not provide any support to its staff when they face problems outside the factory.

viii. Often a new person is appointed who takes over as the head of the section ignoring a number of people within the section with several years of experience.

Workers feel that they are technically more competent than some of their supervisors. In fact some feel that there is no need for supervision in their job. "Work is self correcting, supervision is redundant".

Management Style

Like many family owned companies KDDL to a large extent depends on the collective thinking of a group of senior and trusted employees. We would like to call them as "Significant others", those who are as entrenched as the owner of the business. KDDL has three such individuals.

Significant Others

The three significant people in KDDL are Head of Bangalore operations, pillars of KDDL. Managing Director sounds the general ideas to them and they work at it to make it a practical proposition. While the Managing Director himself takes a lot of decisions, the opinion of these people is always given due consideration. Operational issues have been delegated to these people and domestic sales and marketing is completely handled by two of the 3 significant others. The Managing Director essentially handles international market, "I want to know what I am doing". Though there are dial factories in China and Thailand, these firms have problems dealing with India. KDDL wants to establish market in China. "If you are really competitive you have got to beat the Chinese in China," claims the Managing Director.

Dealing with Managing Director on various issues was not an easy task for the significant others. Managing Director seems to feel very strongly about some issues and wants no differences in opinions. However on other issues a collective belief is evolved. Two examples seem to support this point. Till today people are not convinced whether Derabassi Unit was at all needed. Similarly there were apprehensions about setting up Ethos. However the long association with significant others has brought a level of understanding amongst them.

Managing Business

How does Managing Director go about managing the business? What principles have been evolved to manage the business? While there are differences in perceptions, by and large there are far more areas of agreement between Managing Director and other members of the senior management.

To begin with a five year vision is developed for each unit and there is an annual review to see where the units are heading so that mid-course correction, whenever necessary, could be made. "He is a strong visionary in terms of growth and expansion," said one of the members of significant others. This is further reinforced by desire to seek precise answers, setting clear-cut tasks and targets and follow up to them. Given the nature of business challenge has been more on operations than strategies. As a believer of processes, he feels that when processes are clearly defined people would follow them realising fully well that one hundred percent fool proof processes are difficult to develop. Moreover what is most important is to have people who could develop these processes. Today KDDL lays a lot more emphasis on people and there is a general consensus to take in more people in the organisation. In managing business no compromises have ever been made with the ethics. "No unethical or illegal thing was done and no shortcuts were taken to be sure that nothing would go wrong".

One way to ensure success in business was a belief that the focus should be on the market and things should be kept to a manageable size. Being in the competitive business, KDDL would not have been able to make the kind of progress that it made during the short period if it would have lost its vision of the market. Managing Director has had a conservative way of doing business and believes that, "risks not taken earlier at KDDL have shackled the kind of growth that could have been achieved at KDDL."

Managing People

Much of the success of KDDL can be attributed to newly evolved style of dealing with people. According to one senior manager who has been with KDDL for a along time, a lot of change in the style of working has taken place. Four-five years ago it was a very closed organisation. Decisions were taken at the top and implementation of the decisions was closely monitored. However this has changed a lot. Today they feel that they have lot more freedom available to take their own decisions. Managing Director listens to the problems and suggestions and acts upon them. Sometimes he is even able to tolerate criticism. If at a lower level a decision is taken "which he does not approve, he does not take action but says it should not happen again".

Managing Director believed "I could do the job better than any one else and moreover it was to show that people should not hesitate to do any job". Today this thinking has changed and a lot of work has been delegated to various levels. There is a general view that Managing Director tends to suggest that managers should not come to him for their problem, "Handle it yourself seems to be the mantra."

Evolving consensus is another strategy that seems to be emerging. The management seems to believe in participative decision making and bringing an agreement amongst all. The concept of improvement groups has been introduced. These people visit other factories to get an idea of the role of management and employees. Monthly meetings are also organised to share production targets, quality assurance and meeting deadlines.

Managing Director himself is a very hardworking person. "I really envy the energy he has", said one member of the significant others. Personal relationship is being replaced by professional accountability. "I was afraid to reward people or appreciate them thinking that once you do so, people would get arrogant and would not work. We neither praised nor punished but generally screamed. I am now making a conscious attempt to change my attitude. I can do better than others. People should not hesitate to change. Risk with people has to be taken. People would grow if processes are in order".

One of the weakness in managing people is in discipline management: "Our consequence management has been weak". We are not insisting on planning and accountability but we have accepted collective responsibility. We have to learn to appreciate and also criticise.

Annexures : Case Study -II

Atlas Cycles

Background

Atlas Cycle started way back in 1951 at Sonepat by the grandfather of the present president, Rai Bahadur Janki Das. His three sons were actively involved in the family business, one of them looking after sales, the second after production and the third after general administration. For as long as the grand father was alive, business moved smoothly and without much problems. It was a family managed organisation where the decisions of elders were respected and followed. Not only this, in situations of crisis the younger members of the family had somebody to look upto whose knowledge, wisdom and treatment provided tremendous degree of comfort to them.

Atlas Units

In the beginning Atlas Cycles, as the parent unit was started at Sonepat. But as the business moved, the markets spread, and freight and taxation involved in shipping cycles to other markets increased. The business was on the expansion mode and since UP happened to be the largest market and it provided benefits in terms of unit establishment a second unit of Atlas cycles was set up in Sahibabad, UP. The UP Government offered a 10 years tax holiday as this industry provided employment potential to the resident of UP. With plans for further expansion, a third unit was set up in Gwalior at Malanpur Industrial Area. This plant manufactures bicycles essentially for domestic market, which are sold in complete knock down (CDK) packages to dealers. This factory manufacturs 55 different models of bicycles of which 15% are fancy cycles and 85% are gold line brand. While gold Line moves easily in the market, fancy cycles have not caught up because of lack of fashion consciousness and bad road conditions in India. It has become easier to cater to southern states from this factory. Though earlier south was not a large market it is becoming a big demand territory now. While Atlas was not known as a brand in South, like Hercules and Raleigh, it has started picking up.

Cycles at Atlas Auto Industries, Kondli are fully exported to markets in Srilanka, Bangladesh, China and USA. Atlas Tubes which was initially an offshoot unit started 17 years ago to manufacture steel tubes for Atlas Cycles, today supplies tubes to its own factories as well as to Maruti, Hero Honda, Bajaj and Telco. This factory has recently received ISO 9001 certification.

From initial production capacity of 350 tones, it went to 1700 tones and today manufactures 3000 tones of steel tube every moth.

Cycle is not an excise item. However since Atlas cycles are superior in material and quality, they are about Rs. 75/- more expensive than other cycles in the same range in Indian market. All the units of Atlas combined had annual sales of 200,000 bicycles per month. This came down to 150,000 bicycles during period prior to demerger. By the end of 2004, it is expected to be 300,000 cycles per year.

Export of bicycles has not been of high order because the company as yet has been domestic oriented. All the units together were exporting 5000 bicycles per month until last year, today each unit exports 5000 bicycles per month and the target is to export 15000 bicycles by the year ending 2004.

Demerger

However, soon after the death of the grandfather things started to change. Family members did not think alike. There were differences of opinion, a sense of insecurity prevailed and decisions were postponed. Earlier parent's decisions were never questioned. Now each decision became the focal point of differences of opinions and feelings. The ill feelings became so strong that besides immediate family members other relatives became persons non-gratia. This feeling was summarised when it was pointed out "with blood brothers give and take has to happen but not with cousins." However members of the family realised that to stay competitive something must be done.

At this point of time Earnest Young were appointed to do a total valuation of the assets and divide them in three equal parts. Each of the family members were given full access to the information and a freedom to question the process. This process continued for about three years during which period the organisation went through a rough patch. The business growth took backseat and only routine work was done. Once this phase was over three piles of all assets of equal value were made and handed over to the three families through a draw of lot. The demerger as is known, came into existence on 1st September 2003.

Even before the demerger, family members were controlling one or the other unit under single company, all using different styles of management. Some of these differences were due to differences in the product. However most of them were influenced by the personalities of the family members. This however did not have any downward effect on the units. Demerger gave them the reason as well as an opportunity to run their units in their own image. It also brought a degree of stability as units were brought on a common platform under a single ownership. In addition, domestic and export markets were also divided. The whole of India was divided into three parts and territories were identified on the basis of proximity to the production unit and market potential using the trends in sales during the last three years. The president and joint president (hence forth called Brothers) got Atlas Steel Tubes at Gurgaon, Atlas Cycles at Malanpur, Jankidas Private Limited at Sonepat and Atlas Auto Industries at Kondli. Just recently the brothers have also acquired 50 acres of land in Uttranchal. They plan to develop a full unit there, which will be later merged in to the group.

The domestic markets that came to their share are: Madhya Pradesh, Karnataka, Kerala, Maharashtra, Orissa. The export markets that came to their share are, Srilanka, Bangladesh, Africa, China. While the market territories have already been identified, if one of the sister concers is not able to meet the quota of it's territory, other members of the family chip in.

Brief Biography of the President

In 1953 at Bombay, in Kapur family, the first child a son was born, who was destined to be an achiever. His early schooling was at Modern school, Delhi and he graduated from Hindu College with a BCom. (honours) degree. Though the opportunities for foreign education were available, he decided to stay back and take interest in family business. Married in 1977, with three children he is currently the President of Atlas Cycles. His family has been involved in a number of philanthropic and charity activities including a fully financed school for the blind in RK Puram, New Delhi.

Reflecting upon his life as a growing child, he imbibed the family values of commitment to religion, pious and simple way of life. "I was never given plenty of money to enjoy and I was told to learn to live within means. We were brought up on a tight leash." Another thing that was continually hammered during the growing up was never to abuse the power of money. Being very close to his grandfather, he learnt the value of being supportive to others. Many of his cousins and relatives who managed their share of atlas units use fear, but he found that "the work that can be done by affection, why use fear" concluding his reflection on his life, he said "I am not a perfect person, but as long as I am effective I am happy."

In an attempt to examine the management styles of the brothers, specific issues and concerns and aspirations of employees at Malanpur factory, interviews were conducted with President, Chief General Manager, Head of the Departments, and Head of the Sections. The descriptions based on these interviews are detailed below.

Atlas Cycles, Malanpur

At Malanpur factory 50 workers are regular and another 441 are contract workers. The method of selection is work of mouth, and training is provided at the shop floor by the concerned supervisors. New recruits are taken initially as helpers and they are trained in 3 operations-where they became the expert, 2nd where they are half expert and third as operator. This is done to ensure that in case of absenteeism (which is about 10%) alternates are available. Transport from Gwalior is provided at subsidised rates.

Malanpur unit pays the minimum wages as stipulated by the Madhya Pradesh Government, and it tied up with the piece rate system. This ensures that workers have a facility to make extra money if they work harder or longer. They also work on a time rate system when production stops because of machine failure or any other reason. Annual bonus paid ranges between 18-20% of the basic pay.

Cycle manufacturing is relatively an easy job. At Malanpur, the factory manufactures frames, forks and mudguards. Rest of the parts come from other places. This factory has about 25% of the market share. Product quality being good return rate is about 2%. Wastage rate during production is 0.5%. In fact as mentioned by one of the head of the departments “Malanpur has become the fear of competitors”.

Employee Concerns

Discussion with few workers, HoD’s and HoS’s personnel identified following HR problems in the factory.

i. Business is growing but salary and promotions are not. Performance of the unit is better compared to other units and competitors who incidentally pay higher wages. But the same is not paid to the employees of Atlas.

ii. Employee satisfaction is low. One of the reason is lack of physical security both within and outside the factory. Company support does not come through during such situations as accidents and police cases. Job security is also doubtful.

iii. Employees are lagging behind in technology awarness. There is a need to be trained in new ways of production.

iv. Family entertainment activities are almost non-existent.

v. Gifts given during Deepwalai are same year after year.

vi. Relations with supervisors can be improved. Good performance goes unnoticed and appreciation hardly comes through.

vii. Uniforms are into provide.

While some of their concerns are largely the legacy of the past but "with new management expectations have also gone up."

Management Styles

One of the outstanding features of management styles in Atlas Cycles is the concept of CORE TEAM. While demerger left the workers to work in units where they were employed. There was pick and choose of the senior employees. Choices were essentially based on long-term associations and personal rapport and loyalty.

The senior people moved along with the brothers of the units that came in their share. The brothers collected a team of five professionals one each in HRM, Finance, Productions and Technical, Material and Marketing and so the concept of CORE

TEAM came into being. Members of the core team are trusted people who could be depended upon for decision-making. While they are stationed in Delhi at the cooperate office their jobs keep them very mobile as they keep visiting the 4 units under the brothers. Since the current set up is very new (demerger took place in September 2003) one responsibility of the core team is to look after day-to-day affairs of the 4 units and develop people in these units which has started happening. If number of visits are any indicator of it, as reported by one of the HOD "Core Team used to come 4-5 times a week, now they come 1-2 times a week".

Factories are getting stream lined and systems have been in place. However the need for Core Team will continue because of the expansion activities. Another reason for the formation of core team was the simple fact that the brothers could not physically visit geographically spread out nnits and hence required their representation through members of the Core Team.

It is based on the assumption that if the brothers concentrated on one unit the other would become sick.

The idea of Core Team is similar to the concept of Think Tank. While the individual units are managed by HoD and HoS, in case of problems they call members of the Core Team. They review the situation, collect information and take decisions in consultation with the brothers. If it turns out that the decision is not workable, it is dropped. Sometimes the process is reversed. The brothers may have some ideas, share them with Core Team and either take decisions or drop the idea. Since all the members of the Core Team know the brothers there is unity of understanding.

Summing up the responsibilities of the Core Team, one member of the team said that "though the team consists of professionals in different functions the decisions of the Core Team are based on the comprehsion of totality". The results is that the "bonding and faith has made Core Team so involved that the losses of the company are taken sadly by its members" by and large, polices are formulated by Core Team which then become the guidelines for decision making process. Not only this, the brothers do not question majority of the decisions made by the Core Team. Giving the reasons for such a state of affairs one member claimed "We are pforessionals, Lalawala Kam Nahin Karte Hain."

Besides the concept of the Core Team individual style of management can be characterised in a variety of ways:

i. Dealing with environment is straightforward. "We do nothing under the table" But opportunities are hardly lost. As a result the cost of cycles is slightly higher than others. At the time of demerger the inventories available were 3 crores for Malanpur, 1 crore for Atlas Auto (Kondli), 3 crores for Atlas Tubes, (Gurgaon). Today Malanpur has a turnover of 110 crores and Atals Auto of 25 crores. Al this has come about by sheer hard work and without cutting corners and taking any loans. For the newly acquired land at Uttranchal a term loan is in process.

ii. Since it is a family run organisation, every one has a say in it which of course delays decisions making but decisions have the concurrence of everyone. Respect for elders still prevails in Atlas and is practiced by the brothers. "It is a conservative, safe playing family and likes to sound every one before taking decisions."

iii. China gets its R & D from developed nations, and manufactures them in China and export to European and American markets. Since R & D came from developed nations product acceptance in those markets is very good. Since Atlas does not have its R &D.

Most designs are obtained from China, manufactured in India and sold to foreign markets. "We are copy cats. We get the best from other places and manufacture them in India."

iv. Management does not believe in unionisation. "We are approachable so why go to a third party." The president maves freely at the shop floor and listens to the problem of employees. "I would rather pay Rs. 100 to workers than go for litigation." Once a year a *Preeti Bhoj* is organized where every employee is invited. The brothers spend time during these occasions with workers and listen to them. "We want them to know that we care. Workers are very important to us".

v. The President feels that he has learnt a lot from his uncle who was a father figure to the workers. His uncle was his ideal. So when my workers say that "I remind them of my uncle, I feel good" Respect for elders and their ideals are still the predominanat pillars of the family. Kapur family is docile and very close knit".

vi. Employee turn over is very low. The minimum any employee has served Atlas is 15 years. This is partly due to decision making that is delegated up to a certain level. For major decisions involving funds, finance and investment, decisions are taken by the brothers in consultation with the Core Team. For all other decisions, the brothers are just a approving or sanctioning authority. Only about 1-2% of the decisions had to be reviewed by the brothers but even in those they gave approvals to the decision taken. But the brothers have generally been facilitative in approach and have encouraged people to take decisions in the interest of the organisation so that "the work does not have to stop or wait for me to take a decisions."

Index

A

Absentees 14
Adaptability 66
Administrative heads 57
Administrative systems 62
Advisory group 34
Age 52
Associations 52
Atlas Cycle 36, 108
Authority 28, 50, 83, 109
Autonomy 59

B

Bajaj 24
Behaviour patterns 42
BEL 61
BHEL 61
Birla 24
Board 34, 37, 56, 60
BPO 70, 71, 73, 75
Brain storming 10
Bureaucracy 11
Bureaucratic 116
Business 25

C

Case Study 113
CEO 19, 22, 26, 35, 60, 95
CEO's 59
Chairman 49, 58
Chinese 5
Chinese business systems 112
CMC 89
Collectivism 66
Competition 4
Competitive environment 37
Conglomerate 102
Consultant 81
Consultation 26
Cooperatives 88
Coping strategies 5
Corporate values 97
Cost management 11
Creativity 14, 93
Crompton Greaves 105
Cross-cultural 12, 47
Cultural background 43
Culturalisation 6

Culture 6, 65, 76, 86
Culture-specific systems 44

D

DCM 24, 34
Decision makers 3
Decision making 19, 29, 96
Delegation 37
Dependence 74
Directors 36
Diverse group 43, 97
Diversification 24, 34
Diversity 2, 43, 97

E

Eicher Tractors 34
Employees 41, 80
Empowerment 114
Enterprise 15, 37
Entrepreneurial 90
Entrepreneurial leadership 29
Entrepreneurship 4
Environment 19, 31
Equality 109
Ethical 105
Ethnic groups 36
Executives 46
Expatriate 42, 46

F

Families 90, 107
Family 27, 28, 36, 37
Family Businesses 21, 27, 91
Family culture 42
Family education 87
Family interest 29
Family Managed Businesses 3, 21
Family Managed Enterprises 107
Family Managed Organisations 24
Family member 22, 23, 25, 26, 34, 35
Family members 22, 23, 34
Family owned 89
Family owned businesses 31
Family relationships 31, 33
Family Type Management 30
Family-managed businesses 90
Family-managed organisation 26
Fate 74
Foreign multinationals 43
Functional departments 9

G

GAIL 61
GE 82
General management 55
General Manager 38
Generation 27
Global 44, 55
Global integration 111
Globalisation 113
Governing Board 60
Government 26, 50, 53
Government systems 58
Guna 110

H

Harmony 109
Hidden agenda 29
Hierarchy 19, 82
Hindustan Lever 10
Home office 40, 41, 45, 47
Honesty 109
HR 8

HRD 26, 91, 92, 103, 111, 112
Human Side of Business 14

I

IBM 10, 82, 94, 100
Incremental returns 23
India 2, 17, 35, 55, 82, 86, 98, 106
Indian 48, 84
Indian culture 89
Indian family 27
Indian managers 45, 108
Indian multinationals 92, 100
Indian organisations 2
Indian styles 92
Indian ways 42
Indians 43
Infosys 35
In-groups 23
Innovation 93
Inter-functional 9
Inventory control 10
IT 8, 35

J

Japanese 5
Japanese organisations 101
Job 64, 67, 99
Job Satisfaction 63, 67, 69
Joint family 30

K

Kamla Dials 36
Kasturbhai 24
Knowledge 10, 86
Knowledge management 10
Koreans 5

L

Leaders 84
Leadership 55, 61, 79
Leadership Style 109
LG Electronics 10, 12, 82
LIC 101, 106
Local company 40
Local management 40, 41
Local responsiveness 111
London Business School 27

M

Mafatlals 24
Management 44, 79, 86, 87, 110
Management approaches 30
Management policies 13
Management practices 15, 44, 56, 93, 111
Management schools 83
Management Style 21, 45, 50, 111, 114
Management systems 4, 5, 41, 59, 90
Manager 26
Managerial hierarchy 50
Managerial practices 1, 54, 100
Managerial styles 30, 114
Managerial systems 58, 79
Managers 50
Managing diversity 93, 96
Managing Styles 39
Man-machine relationship 98
Manpower 55
Market 7, 61
Marketing 8
Markets 54
Merit 52

Middle management 112
Ministry 60
MNCs 110
Models 34
Motivational factors 81
MoU 57
Multinational Enterprises 110
Multinationals 3, 19, 20, 39, 42, 45, 47, 48, 91, 92
Multi-unit company 32

N

National Thermal Power Corporation 10
Native employees 46
NTPC 61

O

Obedience 74
Operating managers 33
Operating practices 44, 53
Operating systems 13
Organisation 9, 64
Organisational Culture 63, 65, 86
Organisational practices 5
Organisations 1, 5, 6, 43, 95, 100
Out-groups 23
Owner-executive 38
Owner-manager 38, 91

P

People Development 102
Performance 46
Performance standards 42
Philanthropy 109
Policies 25, 59, 85, 113
Political leadership 51
Positive Leader 103
Power 28
power-orientation 104
Practices 9, 83, 113
process of localization 112
Professional management 36
Professional managers 33
Professionalizing 25
Profitability 54
Promotion 52, 64
PSUs 61, 113, 116
Psychological 103
Public sector enterprises 3, 20, 49, 54, 55, 92
Public sector organisations 54
Public sector undertakings 113

R

R&D 60, 71, 91
Ranbaxy 34
Re-designing jobs 100
Research 2, 27, 47
Review system 32
Risk taking 37
Role 25, 109
Routinisation 30

S

SAIL 61, 104, 105
Samkhya 110
Sarabhai 24
SBI 101, 106
Second 27
Selection procedures 45
Self sacrifice 108
Senior managers 44, 102
Seniority 52
Sharing 108
Skills 13, 87

Social circle 46
Social group 43, 88
Social interaction 46
Social life 98
Social organisation 87
Social status 28
Social-cultural milieu 47
Societal patterns 20
Society 47, 58, 85, 97, 98
Sociologists 99
STC 58
Strategic decisions 33
Strategies 5, 20, 112
Strengths 54
Styles of management 32
Styles of managing 6
Sub-systems 101
Supervision 46, 88
Support systems 13
Supra-manager 22, 32
Systems manager 26

T

Team 31
Technological systems 9
Technology 7, 8, 11, 13, 23, 25, 27, 54
Technology processes 52
Techno-managers 20
Third generation 23
Third generation family 36
Tolerance 83, 96, 108
Top management 113
Trade unions 51
Tradition 31
Traditional families 85
Traditions 86
Training 33, 42, 55
Trust 108
TVS 38, 84

U

Union 51
Upper middle class 43

V

Values 84, 98, 110, 115

W

Weaknesses 54
Wipro 35
Work climate 114
Work environment 31
Work methods 3
Work processes 33
Work system 11
Workers 80, 99

X

Xerox 82